RECOVA RESEARCH
improving business performance

THE HIGH PERFORMANCE ENTERPRISE

A GUIDE TO ENSURING BUSINESS SUCCESS

By
W. KRUZ, A. STRATIGAKIS, G.HUNT

Recova Research
U.S.A.

Order this book online at www.trafford.com
or email orders@trafford.com

Most Trafford titles are also available at major online book retailers.

Print information available on the last page.

ISBN: 978-1-4120-3104-2 (sc)

Trafford rev. 02/11/2020

 www.trafford.com

North America & international
toll-free: 1 888 232 4444 (USA & Canada)
fax: 812 355 4082

TABLE OF CONTENTS

FOUR STEPS TO ACHIEVE THE HIGH PERFORMANCE ENTERPRISE

A Guide To Ensuring Business Success

By

Walter Kruz, Alex Stratigakis, Gerald Hunt

Introduction

The increasingly competitive environment of global trade requires in-depth knowledge and optimum application of enterprise business disciplines to improve profitability and competitive standing. This guide presents a methodology designed to improve business processes and optimize performance of physical assets and human capital thus enabling creation of a competitive advantage.

Four steps are necessary to create the high performance enterprise:

- Business process improvement for cost-effective operations
- Strategy development and implementation for alignment of assets
- Valuation of fixed and intellectual assets for financial visibility
- Continuous improvement and technology adoption

Relentless competitive pressures brought about in part by industrial globalization require extracting every bit of performance from enterprise assets. The high performance enterprise continually aligns strategies, processes and goals while leveraging corporate assets to optimize shareholder value.

It is necessary for the global enterprise, therefore, to possess a management system that effectively integrates people, assets, technologies, and processes into a unified high performance drive toward optimum creation of value for the enterprise.

It is difficult today to conduct a valuation of all tangible and intangible assets since traditional financial reports are based on fixed, or tangible assets. Generally Accepted Accounting Principles (GAAP) have proven insufficient to accurately describe the total financial performance of an enterprise. Ascertaining the value of intangible assets such as intellectual capital, for example, is a problem that remains essentially unresolved.

Our research shows that one obstacle to achieving high performance is the lack of visibility into the true value of the enterprise. Our methodology extends visibility into all enterprise assets, physical and intellectual, beyond that provided by today's financial reporting.

Success of business strategies that emphasize tangible financial results from best practices depends greatly on the implementation of performance measurements that can gauge the ongoing impact of capital investment. This guide takes existing management systems and financial performance measurements as a reference and offers additional insight into developing measurement frameworks and internal financial reporting tools that increase visibility on the performance of enterprise assets.

We call this additional perspective Extended Capital Management (ECM). It answers the management need to focus on the use of resources to create strategic and sustainable value for all stakeholders. The Extended Balance Sheet and the Extended Income Statement are internal reporting tools that provide more visibility into the true value of the firm through the valuation of the firm's intangible assets. They also separate expenses associated with assets that create long-term value from those required to sustain daily operations.

These concepts are presented as a How to Guide for improving financial performance of the firm. It includes guidelines for designing financial measurement frameworks as well as extensive metrics associated with Customer Relationship Management (CRM), Supply Chain Management (SCM), and Intellectual Asset (IA) valuations.

We will present actual performance metrics utilizing management systems such as the Balanced Scorecard (BSC) and value added measures of performance such as Economic Value Added (EVA) to extend their utility into the ECM dimension of performance.

CHAPTER I

1.1 The Role Of Business Process Improvement (BPI) In The High Performance Enterprise

In this chapter, the reader will learn the importance and value of business process analysis and improvement as a major step in creating a high performance enterprise. Various concepts and statistics will explain how process analysis and improvement are key success factors for implementing strategic change and achieving higher business performance. A process improvement methodology is shown in various industrial scenarios the reader will find useful; Six Sigma, Sales and Distribution, and Financial. The chapter closes with the description of an advanced BPI methodology to bring to the reader the latest research on business process improvement.

> *"A tall building can only be built on a sound foundation"*
>
> *-Ancient proverb*

The wisdom of the ancients is still valid today. In the world of business, fortunes have been made and lost because of such a simple proposition.

Present-day global competitive pressures force the enterprise to look at continuous improvement of its operations in order to retain or create a competitive advantage. Research indicates that high operational and financial performance is dependent on the effective design and execution of business processes; in other words, a sound process foundation.

Chrysler Group, the U.S. unit of Germany's DaimlerChrysler lost $1.9 billion in 2001 and three points market share since 1999. In order to recover its market position, Chrysler has revamped its design and manufacturing processes in what may be Detroit's largest collaborative design and engineering project to date. Chrysler's goal is to improve quality and lower production costs [1].

5

A firm, such as Chrysler or any other, can be viewed as a collection of internal business processes. Its financial performance is therefore determined by the effective interaction of those processes producing the desired outcomes.

Authors Hammer and Champy defined a business process in their book "Reengineering the Corporation" as "a collection of activities that takes one or more kinds of input and creates an output that is of value to the customer".

From our perspective, we will define business processes as the set of activities a firm performs to create value for its stakeholders. These activities are carried out across organizations and can be decomposed into the detailed tasks necessary to fulfill its mission. One example is the order fulfillment process and another, the software quality assurance process. More precisely, from a performance perspective, business processes include elements of:

- Organization

  Consists of the functional divisions that produce and facilitate the delivery of a product or service. One goal toward high performance is to flatten the organization overall. (Sample performance measurement: Average number of employees per manager)

- Processes

  Consist of all tasks and activities that create and deliver the product or service. A goal here is lower cost through efficiencies. (Sample performance measurement: Cost of Goods Sold)

- Technology

  Includes all technical wherewithal utilized in creating the product or service. A goal in this area is to align the technologies being used to support the firm's business strategy. (Sample performance measurement: IT cost per employee)

- People

    Includes all stakeholders of the firm. The overall goal is to create value for the firm. A tactical goal is to maximize the value of the intellectual capital represented by the employees. (Sample performance measurement: Ratio of Advanced Degrees in the firm)

When working with software tools for model analysis and simulation as we shall see in later chapters, we can leverage Davenport and Short [2] who defined processes in terms of dimensions:

- **Entities**: Processes take place between organizational entities. They could be inter-organizational, as in the extended enterprise when dealing with external processes. (Logistic processes).

- **Objects**: Processes result in manipulation of objects. These objects could be physical or informational and possess user-defined attributes.

- **Activities**: Processes could involve types of activities: Managerial (signature approval), and Operational (testing an integrated circuit).

The enterprise seeks to integrate processes and all other assets to optimize its performance. A simple representation of a high performance enterprise could be made in the form of a triangle, as in Exhibit 1, where the integration of processes with people skills, intellectual assets, and technologies results in high performance organizations that continuously create value for the firm's shareholders.

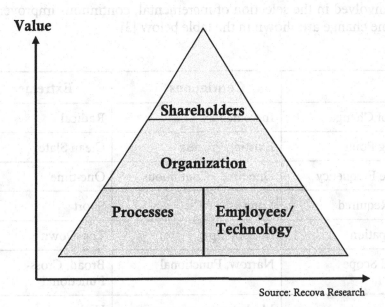

Exhibit 1. The High Performance Enterprise

Prior to implementing any major strategic changes, the enterprise needs to foster a necessary debate involving the speed and extent of change necessary to achieve its objectives. Firms that have successfully integrated information technology tools (IT) into their processes show a continuing reduction in their design and product development cycles. Competitive strategies nowadays require increasingly faster internal response and improvement for maintaining a competitive advantage.

Total Quality Management (TQM), a continuous improvement methodology in vogue in the early 90s emphasized continuous incremental improvement of processes and organizations. Business Process Reengineering (BPR), and lately Extreme Business Reengineering as proposed by author Champy, involves discrete initiatives resulting in radical improvement in short periods of time.

Research shows that both approaches are valid in different contexts. While significant changes may be required to create a competitive advantage or to meet a competitor's threat of a new line of products and features, a policy of continuous improvement is appropriate for sustaining that advantage over the long term or until a suitable technology option is available.

Factors involved in the selection of incremental, continuous improvement or extreme change are shown in the table below [3].

	Continuous	**Extreme**
Level of Change	Incremental	Radical
Starting Point	Existing Process	Clean Slate
Change Frequency	One-time /Continuous	One-time
Time Required	Long	Short
Participation	Bottom-Up	Top-Down
Typical Scope	Narrow, Functional	Broad, Cross-Functional
Risk	Moderate	High
Primary Enabler	Statistical Control	Information Technology
Type of Change	Cultural	Cultural/Structural

Source: Davenport

Exhibit 2. Incremental Improvement versus Extreme Business Reengineering

The Chrysler improvement of its design methodology is a good example showing elements of both incremental and Extreme Business Reengineering [8]. The level of change includes heavy application of internet technologies and e-business methods to create new products; this required cultural and structural adjustments. The implementation risk was moderate in that, although relatively new, other industry leaders have used similar internet and e-commerce methods as utilized at Chrysler. The starting point was from existing processes -not from a clean slate. The scope of change was broad; it included product design processes as well as financial management, change management, and prototype procurement. The time span for the bulk of this effort was two years. The common business improvement method seen in industry appears to be a combination of both incremental and fast-paced change, as required by the competitive landscape, and budgetary and organizational constraints.

1.2 Why Are Business Processes Important?

Products and services create value for a firm. A firm, as indicated above, is a collection of business processes that are linked across the enterprise. This linkage crosses many organizational boundaries until it reaches the customer and has a direct impact on customer satisfaction and operational costs. Weak processes increase cost, lower quality, and reduce customer satisfaction. In other words, poor processes create low value for the firm.

Industry examples where successful companies emphasize the soundness of their business processes to achieve high performance are numerous. According to the San Jose Mercury News [4]; while facing the telecommunications industry slowdown of 2001, Cisco Systems "wrote off $2.2 billion in inventory, and an additional $1.1 billion for layoffs...The company went through a major reorganization of its internal processes, its IT systems, its operation, and its culture." In November 2003, Cisco reported its first quarter of revenue growth in three quarters, as well as improved visibility in terms of positive growth. Clearly, this is a case where a firm needed to re-assess and revamp its processes and strategy execution to deal with a changing environment.

In pursuing customer satisfaction, for example, all elements of the organization must work together to ensure that processes cutting across organizational boundaries are indeed effective. Because of the lack of appropriate tools, firms have, even today, taken a single-dimensional view of process interactions typically limited to single departments. Second-order effects of process interactions are only now beginning to be addressed by few firms through computer-aided tools.

Organizations, both in the private and government sectors, utilize a large number of processes in pursuit of their mission. The scope of these processes is very complex cutting through functional and hierarchical levels of the organization. The supply chain management process alone adds even more complexity because it deals with external processes belonging to suppliers, distributors, customers, and government. These quickly become unwieldy and out of alignment with the organization's business objectives. In this case, improvement will only take place in very small increments due to the lack of visibility into the complete set of relationships included in the process. In effect, no one really understands the whole process.

A 2003 survey of American companies by CFO Research Services showed that business process improvement is still an afterthought for most companies. Of the high tech companies surveyed, only 29% assessed processes before system implementation. Most either implemented technology and process changes simultaneously (44%), or after the fact (27%), if necessary.

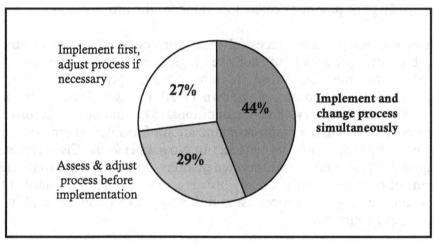

Source: CFO Research Services

Exhibit 3. Few Companies Adjust Processes Before Implementation

Optimization of business processes (BPI) can have a profound effect in the performance of an organization. Typically, these effects translate into:

- Cost reduction

  As processes are analyzed and made more efficient, duplication of effort is eliminated, inefficient handling of activities is improved, and consolidation of similar tasks is often possible. The immediate benefit of these improvements is in terms of lower transactional cost and reduced use of resources for a given task.

- Value added

  Improved understanding of existing processes leads to improvements that are more customer-focused and in better alignment with the organization's mission. This may occur independent of other strategic implementations, such as the Balanced Scorecard.

- Reduced time to market

  More efficient execution of processes implies a reduction in the time required for their completion. This is especially evident in product design and development where concurrent engineering is an effective way to reduce design and development cycles.

- Reduction of risk

  The ability of advanced business process analysis and simulation enables firms to test alternative models prior to their implementation thus increasing the chance of success for any given process and reducing implementation risk. These models are validated against existing performance metrics; as a result, performance targets become more realistic.

- Identification of best practices

  Continuous improvement of business processes enables staff to identify practices most applicable to a business model. These best practices go a long way toward improving performance while improving customer satisfaction and reducing costs. In this manner, innovation is integrated into the business model and the firm can safely move toward early adoption of suitable technologies.

Clearly, process improvement is a first step in achieving high performance for the enterprise. By itself, this is a high value but complex undertaking. After all, just a medium size enterprise performs hundreds of thousands of activities to deliver its product to customers; the scope of a project could quickly be overwhelming. Is there a way to formalize a BPI approach to take advantage of it in an industrial setting?

Methodology utilized by Six Sigma quality programs offers guidance in this regard [5]. Six Sigma is a management approach that quantifies and solves problems and optimizes critical business processes. Research shows that Six Sigma programs can result in significant improvements in business performance and profitability. In a manufacturing environment, a Six Sigma program would typically focus in reducing the number of defects in a subassembly. In a service environment, it would focus in reducing the number of product returns, for example.

Some Six Sigma quality programs are implemented according to the following phases: Define, Measure, Analyze, Implement, and Control. We can translate these phases directly into a business process improvement methodology:

Six Sigma	BPI	Goal
Define	Process Identification	Prioritize Critical Issues
Measure	Process Documentation	Quantification of Issue
Analyze	Process Analysis	Evaluate Options
Improve	Process Implementation	Validate Benefits
Control	Continuous Improvement	Ensure Performance

Exhibit 4. BPI Methodology

Process identification selects the most impacting issues in terms of benefits. Not all processes utilized by the enterprise need to be addressed; only those offering the most benefit for the time and resource investment.

Process documentation enables a collaborative effort where all the stakeholders of a given process or issue can work with the same set of information. Representation of the process can take the form of simple work flow diagrams to complex computer-aided models available for real-time testing by multiple contributors.

Process Analysis takes information from users to examine the strengths and weaknesses of a given process and develop alternatives. Computer-aided analysis allows the development and testing of multiple alternatives for second order effects, thus increasing model accuracy.

Implementation of the new and improved process takes place after a satisfactory model has been approved. Beta performance testing of the model reduces implementation risk. Continuous improvement of the new process takes advantage of the new awareness created by this project and incorporates ongoing feedback from users for further optimization. Ongoing feedback could include technology options, as they become available.

1.3 Technology Adoption And Process Improvement For Enhanced Performance

Business process improvement and information technologies (IT) go hand in hand in raising performance of the enterprise. Sound business processes that utilize IT tools go a long way toward creating a competitive advantage. Judging from Exhibit 3, that indicated only 29% of firms assess and adjust changes before system implementations, a firm with a sound process foundation has a good chance at leaving the competition behind when adopting new technologies. Such an example is presented below by the Pepsi case study [6].

1.3.1 The Pepsi Case Study

The Pepsi case study deals with the transformational impact of technology in improving performance of a business model. From a static, inefficient, and costly model, wireless technology adoption enabled PepsiCo to significantly improve its way of doing business in the areas of Sales and Brand Management, Delivery and Inventory management, and Pricing and Billing Consistency. The results included lower costs, increased customer satisfaction, and increased efficiency and visibility into the business.

As background, PepsiCo, Inc. is a world leader in the convenient foods and beverages industry. Its Sales and Distribution model in a given regional area consisted of drivers delivering soft drinks to customers in prescribed routes. The quantity of drinks the drivers loaded their trucks were based on a best guess of customer's needs. The drivers invoiced customers for their purchases and returned undelivered inventory as well as damaged goods to the warehouse that evening. That operation carried a significant operational costs. For decades, this "best guess delivery" with all its inefficiencies (wrong and insufficient deliveries, stock-outs) and high cost was the accepted way of doing business. Tough competition forced PepsiCo to do something different. The results are described in the tables below.

14

The Problem

The number of products to be delivered eventually surpassed delivery capabilities and stores' shelf space. Sales suffered as delivery agents struggled to handle the new loads and differentiate brands.

The Solution

Pepsi's largest bottlers moved to separate the Sales from the Delivery jobs. Wireless technology was adopted to enable Salespeople to pre-sell orders, differentiate brands, and win better store shelf placement. The drivers now were able to load and deliver the right products, in the right quantities, to the right customer, saving millions of dollars in time and wasted inventory.

The Result

Lower cost per case of soda sold; increased sales of products in the Pepsi mix.

Exhibit 5. Improvement in the Sales and Brand Management Area

The Problem

Delivery quantities were based on the driver's best guess of customer needs. This led to overstocks sometimes as high as 50%. Customers also complained of frequent out-of-stocks incidents.

The Solution

Orders taken from salespeople are now relayed immediately back to the plant through wireless devices. Next day deliveries are planned in exact quantities and for an optimized route. Drivers can now respond to last minute route changes.

The Result

Overstock and damage rates have decreased up to 30% on some routes; under-stocks are declining on test routes.

Exhibit 6. Improvement in the Delivery and Inventory Management Area

Improved business processes supported by a key technology, wireless communications, made a powerful solution to the problem described in exhibit 5 and established a new level of performance for the company. Wireless communications is a particularly effective technology that enables business performance improvements in many areas. Application of this technology can take many forms, from simple cell phone applications to sophisticated real-time GPS tracking systems for fleet management.

PepsiCo extracted a great deal of business performance benefit as this case shows, among them:

- **Improved fleet visibility**

  The Distribution department could now locate every truck on the field and optimize their utilization as new and updated orders took place.

- **Delivery productivity**

  Truckers were now focused on delivering the right orders to the right customers at the right time. Missed deliveries and wrong orders were essentially eliminated increasing the efficiency and effectiveness of the operation.

- **Improved communications**

  Sales and Delivery employees, now dedicated to single functions, focused on their respective functions and improved the effectiveness of communications among these two groups. A degree of automation reduced the paperwork and improved the accuracy of field reports.

The Problem

Salespeople might sell a product to a customer who is not authorized to buy, or at a price that headquarters has not approved.

The Solution

Improved wireless access to headquarters database for price and product configurations significantly reduce error rate. At the same time, a single marketing message is delivered to customers improving chances for satisfaction.

The Result

Faster and more targeted introduction of new products, fewer invoice discrepancies, and increased cross selling of products for higher volumes and revenue.

Exhibit 7. Improvement in Pricing and Billing Consistency

1.4 Improving Financial Processes For Enhanced Performance

Financial reports are notorious as laggard indicators of business performance; it is not unlike driving while looking only at the rearview mirror. It would be of much value to a firm to also look at leading indicators of performance to better see the road ahead. This is now possible through computer-based advancements in the area of business process analysis. Dynamic simulation of business models, as one example, combined with financial tools can provide the forward visibility the enterprise has lacked heretofore. Improved forward financial visibility enables management to anticipate and respond to business trends ahead of the competition. The ability to respond quicker and better to a changing market has a direct effect on competitiveness.

Financial measurements of performance focus naturally on the easier to visualize fixed assets of the enterprise. However, a major portion of the value of a firm lies in its non-fixed assets such as intellectual property (patents, research), branding, and customer satisfaction, among many others.

Valuation of these assets will be discussed in later chapters of this book; for now we will concentrate on the ability to adjust business processes to enhance the value of these assets.

Computer aided business process analysis facilitates the testing of multiple what-if cases. A fairly static process such as budgeting can be optimized through the modeling of alternative scenarios that validate not only the logical integrity of these various approaches but also their performance through financial metrics. Existing metrics from various enterprise systems serve to validate a model's feasibility and provide a constant sanity check.

The multidimensional nature of dynamic modeling facilitates a collaborative approach to developing new models for budgeting, for example, whereby the firm's intranet could be the facilitating medium for distribution. Many stakeholders can input their own scenario into a development or scenario database that calculates this input into the overall targets for the firm. This can be particularly useful in evaluating changes related to proposed consolidations, outsourcing, new product releases, and others.

Multidimensional dynamic simulation also promotes the integration of non-financial measures in this analysis. Performance measures such as customer satisfaction, perfect orders, and employee retention can be included to enhance the forward financial visibility of alternatives. The computer-based nature of simulations allows testing secondary or downstream effects on operations that would normally go unnoticed. We are intuitively aware that an apparent optimum revenue model might have a negative effect on some operations. A cost reduction on a manufacturing assembly, for example, could increase product returns, and by extension, reduce customer satisfaction.

Balanced Scorecard implementations can benefit to a great extent by the use of this methodology. Two major reasons for balanced scorecard implementation failures, according to research, are first, poor business processes that could not support strategic initiatives and second, failure to identify and develop suitable performance measures. Simulation can address both issues equally well. As explained earlier in this chapter, processes can be simulated, quickly and at minimum cost until a suitable model is developed. Part of this analysis includes developing associated performance metrics for every alternative model. This means that every model can be validated for financial performance against existing metrics.

The overall effect of simulation is to provide increased visibility into the financial performance of alternative models, to optimize the various layers of interactions created by changes in the business, and to communicate enterprise-wide how and by how much every organization is going to support the firm's strategy. This is a powerful capability indeed to help achieve the next level of performance for the enterprise.

1.5 An Advanced Business Process Improvement Methodology

Recent advances in the connectivity of a firm with suppliers and customers as shown in the e-business area, has created complexities that require new business process analysis methodologies. One such technology is dynamic simulation, the ability to create computer-based business model prototypes that can be tested for a variety of scenarios. This capability allows the firm to test changes and measure their financial impact prior to implementation.

Business process analysis (BPA) and simulation allows representation of processes, people, and technology in a dynamic computer model.

A model, when simulated, recreates the operations of a business in a software environment. This is accomplished by executing the operations in compressed time while displaying a graphical representation of the workflow. Because simulation software produces statistics about model changes, performance of an individual process, and potentially a large organization, can be evaluated by analyzing the model data.

Tools of various complexities and capabilities are rather plentiful for analysis and simulation of business models. These software tools enable the user to graphically document business processes, organizations, and hierarchical management structures. The user can associate these graphical elements through logical rules, treating a process or activity as software objects that can be manipulated and changed as required. In addition, the simulation tool normally supports sensitivity analysis by allowing rapid changes to the model logic and data. The most powerful tools for business process simulation utilize a discrete event-driven simulation approach.

Typically, an internal database capability stores and archives the models under study allowing a knowledge database and collaborative involvement by the organization. For effective leverage of these tools, the output models can be published in the intranet as part of the firm's internal documentation. This facilitates regulatory compliance as audits (ISO 9000) can now be conducted in real-time, that is, as a regularly scheduled internal activity rather than an occasional and expensive exercise.

Simulation enables a cost-effective evaluation of practical scenarios in support of strategic initiatives or in support of continuous improvement efforts. Examples of such evaluations are in New Product Introduction (NPI), manufacturing throughput, and improved customer response times.

A description of a dynamic business process simulation methodology [7] follows:

- **Capture the AS IS process dynamically**

  Provides in-depth understanding of existing operations for all stakeholders. Simple workflow diagrams show organizations, people, interactions, and associated metrics in a multidimensional model that enhances visibility of internal processes and their mutual interactions.

- **Validate the AS IS model**

  ➢ Internal automated logic validation checks all process linkages preventing errors. Earlier tools would allow errors to remain undetected.

  ➢ The model accuracy is validated against existing metrics. Existing metrics from actual operations provide a basis for comparison and a sanity check.

- **Design and test TO BE model**

  Test business model prototypes and measure expected benefits in terms of revenue and productivity to ensure effort will achieve business objectives. Computer-based simulation tests any number of parameters and what-if cases. Existing metrics provide validation source for new performance targets.

- **Persuasively communicate proposed changes**

  Stakeholders review and approve changes that are created by the stakeholder team. The new model can be published on the Intranet as the new model is created. This is an important part of the collaborative discipline imposed by this methodology and an effective way to align resources with strategy.

- **Provide a dynamic framework for implementation and change management**

  Ease of analysis and simulation makes this process dynamic and responsive to market changes. Rapid incorporation of new information, new capabilities, and new technologies provide the basis for continuous improvement.

Application of this methodology provides assurance that:

- The firm's internal and external processes have been reviewed and improved where necessary. Inefficiencies and duplication have been removed.

- Enterprise assets are now better utilized, their use has been optimized, and they are now better aligned for more effective support of the business strategy.

- A new core competence, BPI, and a culture of proactive and continuous improvement enable the firm to respond quickly and effectively to changes in the business environment.

Today's Extended Enterprise is connected through a network of relationships including suppliers, internal processes, customers, and partners. These relationships or linkages create process complexities that require the use of sophisticated process improvement methodologies. We shall see later in this Guide, that some performance metrics become composite metrics, especially where internal and external elements to the firm are linked.

In summary, continuous improvement of business processes, as a minimum, removes the burden of operational inefficiencies and opens the possibility of transformational change thereby enhancing the enterprise's capability to create value for its stakeholders. As part of a successful performance improvement methodology, it is important to lay first a strong process foundation upon which any systems, methods, or new technologies can deliver optimum results.

In completing this chapter, the reader became familiar with business process improvement methodologies and how they are applied in an industrial environment to improve the financial performance of the enterprise. We examined the benefits of BPI in terms of Six Sigma and Balanced Scorecard requirements and learned pitfalls of BSC implementations the reader can now avoid. We also examined the concepts of dynamic simulation and its power to expand visibility into alternative models for improvement. With the simple concepts presented here and in the ensuing chapters, the reader can develop a suitable roadmap that he or she can leverage to build the strong foundation required to improve the firm's business performance.

References:

[1] *Business Week Magazine*, September 2, 2002.
[2] T.H., "Process Innovation", *Harvard Business School Press*, 1993.
[3] Davenport, T.H. & Short, J.E., "IT and BPR," *Sloan Management Review*, 1990.
[4] *San Jose Mercury News*, December 11, 2003.
[5] "The Role of Process Modeling Within Six Sigma", Micrografx *Inc*, 2002.
[6] "The Pepsi Case Study", *CIO Insight Magazine*, April 2003.
[7] Recova Research, www.recova.com, 2003.
[8] J. Champy, "X-Engineering the Corporation", 2003.

CHAPTER II

2.0 Strategy Development And Implementation

In this chapter, the reader will learn the role that strategy development and implementation plays in ensuring high business performance. We will review the components of strategy development and implementation to help those involved in such efforts. We will also examine the pitfalls of strategy implementation and leverage the benefits of the Balanced Scorecard methodology such as strategy maps to link a business vision to the individual contribution of employees. We will become acquainted with the deficiencies of today's financial systems in recognizing intangible assets, a major inhibitor of performance, and offer ways to resolve that issue.

"If you know the enemy and know yourself, you need not fear the result of one hundred battles.... "

Sun Tsu in The Art of War

The development and execution of business strategies based on knowledge about competitors is essential to raising performance of the organization. High performance can be achieved when a clear vision has been defined and communicated to stakeholders, when strategic planning anticipates trends, threats, and opportunities, and when the resulting strategies are designed to build a sustainable competitive advantage.

Creating and communicating a vision is to take a proactive approach at determining the future of the business. A clear vision provides the basis of an effective and motivating *esprit de corps* that serves as a personal performance reminder for the individual. A vision, unlike goals and objectives, sets a long term, simplified view of the business. An example is Cisco Systems' John Chambers, "In today's environment, it's all about getting back to the basics in terms of focusing on the areas that a company can influence and control: cash generation, available market share gains, productivity increases, profitability and technology innovation. These factors will ultimately determine who will survive in this challenging economy." [1]

A great deal of commitment and hard work is required to bring a vision to fruition. A vision needs to be supported by strong leadership, effective business strategies, and core competencies. Strategies need to be decomposed into actionable items, and the people carrying out tactical assignments need to believe in the vision and possess the necessary skills for effective implementation.

Exhibit 1 visualizes the decomposition of a vision into the actionable items or tasks that will make that vision a reality. These elements generally include:

- **Mission**

  The business' reason for being is characterized by its mission. A brief statement indicating the purpose of a business in terms of its impact on customers, products or services, and stakeholders is known as a mission statement. It focuses the stakeholders toward meeting common objectives.

- **Business Values**

  They address the norms of behavior by the firm in relation to its stakeholders, competition, and society at large.

- **Business Strategies**

  They define the way the vision and mission will be fulfilled and provide focus and direction to enterprise level efforts. They may specifically define business targets such as percentage of market share in sectors of interest or define directions of growth.

- **Business Objectives**

  They state the overall goals required for success in terms of results in the areas of profitability, quality, market share, and any applicable element of the business environment.

  They are specific in setting targets of performance for functional areas such as product quality, manufacturing output, and cost containment. They will also specify the time frames in which these goals need to be accomplished.

- **Projects**

  A set of tasks to be addressed collaboratively and in support of a business strategy.

- **Tasks**

  The individual work assignments an employee undertakes in support of a project or a functional activity. Typically, working at this level the employee has lost visibility of the business strategies being deployed due to poor communications or lack of interest. Performance is left to individual initiative and may or may not link with the objectives of the organization.

Ideally, however, all the elements involved in a strategic initiative are linked to one another in a continuous fashion and mutually support each other in the fulfillment of their individual functions. We could think of it as a strategy wheel where the hub and spokes connect different elements that work together to move the enterprise forward.

Exhibit 1 portrays a continuous and collaborative linkage among all these elements where every employee is actively working in support of the business strategies. Broken linkages result in inefficiencies, greater than anticipated costs, missed targets, lower morale, and ultimately, failed strategies. A common post-mortem finding when analyzing failed strategies is that the human component has not been addressed correctly thus allowing it to become a significant factor in that failure.

The Strategy Wheel

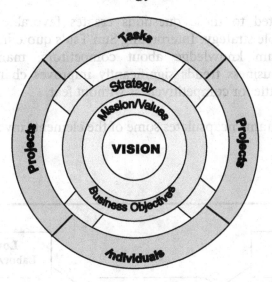

Exhibit 1. Enterprise Linkages of a Strategy

2.1 Developing A Global Strategy

Today's competitive environment requires a firm to develop or conform to a global strategy. A global strategy needs to consider the following elements. [2]:

- Locations where products and services will be offered
- Market share for products and services across those locations
- Degree of standardization for products and services across countries
- Location of value-added activities such as research and production
- Degree of standardization for brand names and marketing activities across locations

- Degree of integration of local strategies with the overall global strategy for the firm

The analysis related to these questions creates favorable conditions for developing a suitable strategy. Interpreting Sun Tsu's quote in business terms; possessing optimum knowledge about competitors, market conditions, regulations, and business trends significantly improves chances for success allowing one to battle for competitiveness without fear.

The following diagram encapsulates some of the elements involved in crafting a global strategy.

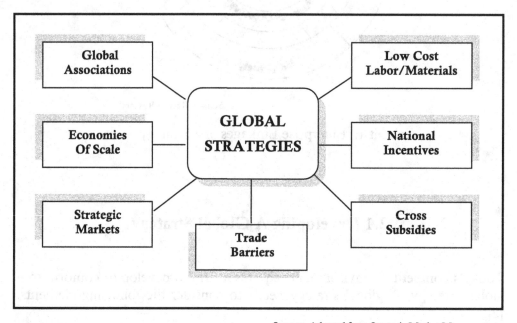

Source: Adapted from Strategic Market Management

Exhibit 2. Elements of a Global Strategy

These elements are representative of the ones found in a global environment and may be more or less applicable in different situations.

Economies of Scale

Economies of scale occur when a product is mass-produced resulting in lower average cost. Economies of scale may originate from a combination of efficient operations, product standardization, low labor cost, and thoughtful use of investment capital.

Access to Low-Cost Labor or Materials

Offshoring, the process of moving manufacturing or service operations from the U.S. to China or India is a manifestation of the search for lower operational cost by American firms. This is a continuing process, one that has gone on for centuries, whereby firms continuously seek a cost advantage over competitors.

Trade Barriers

Trade agreements are a good example of reducing trade barriers. NAFTA, The North American Free Trade Agreement signed by the United States, Canada, and Mexico has been instrumental in substantially increasing trade among these countries due to lower barriers. Similarly, foreign automotive manufacturers have installed assembly plants in the U.S. and Europe to reduce the bias against foreign cars in those countries and to ensure access to those markets.

Access Strategic Markets

Sizable markets such as the U.S and Europe are strategic because of their size, technology, and innovation capability. Access to these markets will ensure availability of up-to-date information in terms of business trends, proximity to innovation, as well as access to specialized skills and research strategic to the firm.

Cross-Subsidies

A firm can subsidize a competitive battle, from profits generated somewhere else, to gain an advantage. A favorite business school case refers to the attempt by Michelin, in the 70s, to attack Goodyear's market share in the U.S. Goodyear was expected to reduce prices or increase advertisement expenditures to counter Michelin's move. Goodyear, however, decided to attack Michelin in its home market in Europe, which resulted in reduced earnings for Michelin.

Create Global Brand Associations

Brand names benefit from associations with global strategies. Mercedes-Benz is a universally recognized name for quality and reliability; Mercedes' new products benefit from a recognized worldwide standard of quality and customers see the brand name as assurance of a value purchase.

Access to Local Government Incentives

Governments around the world offer a variety of incentives to attract foreign manufacturing facilities. Incentives range from tax holidays to land and building subsidies that may generate a cost advantage for the firm. Chinese cities in a development region are known to offer subsidies and lower tax regimes for companies considering a move to their especially built high technology parks.

2.2 Implementing Strategies

Developing strategies is but the first step of a long march. Implementing such strategies is a much harder task; the business arena is strewn with failed attempts. Here is a summary of failure causes tabulated by functional areas. [3]

Finance	Management	Marketing & Sales	Products & Services	Operations
Underestimating start-up costs for operations and capital expenditure	Insufficient experience in that sector	Misjudging the size or growth of the overall market	Inability to supply profitably at required price	Under-investment in equipment, facilities, etc.
Insufficient funds or access to top-up finance	Insufficient functional breadth	Overoptimistic estimates of market penetration and shares	Problems with maintaining quality standards	Excessive overhead relative to scale of operations
Wrong mix of funds (e.g. too much debt and gearing too high)	Inability to communicate strategy and secure commitment	Delays in securing or developing distribution channels	Restricted range of offerings	High operational costs and/or low productivity
Over reliance on trade credit (receivables)	Unrealistic expectations	Underestimating the strength of competitors	Lack of innovation (me-too products)	Poor capacity utilization
Mistaking profit for cash flow	No formal or clear structures	Misreading customer requirements	Problems securing third-party supplies	Inadequate physical distribution
Overoptimistic financial projections	Ineffective financial and managerial control systems	Lack of promotion and customer awareness	Offerings out of line with customer needs	Inadequate physical distribution
Unable to withstand interest rate increases.	Lack of management accountability	Inability to handle an economic slowdown.		

Source: Adapted from www.planware.org

Exhibit 3. Causes of Failed Strategy Implementations

In the case of the People's Republic of China (PRC) strategic options for economic development, some business literature indicates that China's comparative advantage of low labor cost is sufficient as a strategy to ensure economic growth and that investment in high technology areas is ill advised [4]. We believe a more suitable strategy for long term economic growth would not rely on a single factor, in this case, low labor cost. A sound strategy would anticipate the early dilution of that advantage by neighboring nations. We would consider two phases of economic development where the PRC:

- Has ensured a first phase of long-term economic development based on the comparative advantage of low labor cost

- And where a second phase of economic development is based on:
  - Greater content of technology for products and services in aerospace, electronics, and medical industries
  - Greater quality standards for products and services in all industries
  - Improved global management skills for business leaders for addressing sustainable growth and development

2.3 One Strategy Implementation Approach, The Balanced Scorecard (BSC)

There is no single management approach for ensuring successful implementation of business strategies. Over time, fashionable approaches come and go and their jargon rises and falls like skirt hemlines. Business school case studies show that intangibles such as timing and vision play a key role in creating success. Most management methodologies have merit, however, so that one must mix and match elements of different approaches that are suitable to the firm's specific set of needs.

At this time, major firms utilize an influential management approach that presents a holistic methodology for performance improvement. This is known as the Balanced Scorecard.

The Balanced Scorecard, initially developed by authors Robert Kaplan and David Norton in the early 1990s, provides a performance management framework that aligns strategy with management processes and systems. A set of measurements quantify that alignment and provide a balanced view of the business. The strategy map, as presented in the book, "The Strategy-focused Organization" by Kaplan and Norton, consists of four perspectives; customer, financial, internal, and learning and growth, that link strategy to actual goals and performance measurements. It is from these perspectives that strategic initiatives are derived each with specific measures, or metrics, to gauge their progress and relative contribution to the business.

The BSC is useful because of its emphasis in creating performance measures that produce accountability at all levels in supporting the business strategy. It also contributes a great deal of value in consolidating enterprise efforts to achieve improved performance and has been implemented successfully by many large companies over the last decade. Enough industry reports however indicate sufficient failure rates to take pause and examine the reasons for failure.

Research indicates that BSC implementations fail mainly due to basic reasons:

- **Weak business processes**

  Business processes that have not been optimized make a poor foundation for any management system implementation. This is a problem that is endemic to industry and is a limiting factor to financial performance under any circumstances [5]. As indicated in Chapter 1, a sound foundation of business processes is a prerequisite for implementation of any strategic plans.

- **Lack of well-defined metrics**

  Identifying the right non-financial measures is always a critical factor for successful implementation of a scorecard. Ideally, performance metrics would provide forward financial visibility to better respond to market changes. Development of effective metrics remains an art and a science.

  Gartner Research believes, "the introduction of a proven framework of standard indicators of performance—a set of specific metrics that are clearly defined and comparable across almost every kind of company and business unit —is needed to solve the problems caused by this "missing link" in the Balanced Scorecard". [6]

- **Insufficient Business Intelligence capabilities or strategy**

  Balanced scorecard implementations often fail because the underlying business intelligence is weak or missing; industry has not yet mastered the transformation of data into information and knowledge. Appropriate business intelligence capabilities will enable management to evaluate the relevance and effectiveness of the parameters being monitored and to develop alternatives more in sync with the strategic direction as changes are necessary.

- **Laws and regulations**

  Government, laws and regulations, environmental groups and other societal groups can impact the organization significantly if the issues at hand are not adequately addressed. Furthermore, if the above are not taken into account when designing the scorecard, a distorted picture of reality emerges that can lead to non-realization of the strategy. [8]

As a management system dealing with decomposing strategies into actionable items, the BSC should not be expected to provide the specific performance measures required for a successful implementation. This is left to the firm's practitioners who are in the best position to understand the variables affecting the business and the historical performance the new metrics will link to.

The table below shows a surprisingly low percentage of companies utilizing a unified source of metrics, such as the BSC, for evaluating financial performance. From these data, it appears that most firms measure enterprise performance as a set of independent efforts and not as a unified set of linkages all supporting a single view of the business. High performance requires all processes and assets working in unison. The lack of a unified strategy and common business objectives will leave the firm vulnerable to changes in the marketplace.

Proportion of firms using scorecards or dashboards to monitor metrics in the following categories	
Sales	21.1%
Finance	18.8%
Customer Service	14.3%
Manufacturing/Operations	12.0%
Supply Chain	10.5%
Human Capital	8.3%

Source: Business Finance Magazine, June 2003

Exhibit 4. Proportion of Firms Using BSC to Monitor Metrics

With this information in mind we expect a scorecard implementation will produce two basic and key business deliverables; on-going accountability for all individuals in the enterprise and performance metrics producing forward business visibility.

- **Ongoing enterprise accountability**

    A unified view of the business where strategies are decomposed into the goals and objectives individual employees will carry out. The linkage between high level strategies and daily activities must produce accountability at all levels of the organization that can be monitored and improved over time.

- **Forward financial visibility**

    Effective metrics that have the effect of measuring the value created by both fixed and intellectual assets. This improved visibility will the basis for continuous financial improvement enabling the enterprise to anticipate and better respond to market changes.

34

2.4 Business Perspectives And Measurements Of The BSC

In their book "The Strategy-focused Organization", Kaplan and Norton make use of different perspectives in arriving at measurements that can effectively gauge the degree to which assets are being utilized in support of strategies. Exhibit [5] extrapolates on Kaplan and Norton's original perspective definitions and shows how they link to the business vision to fulfill.

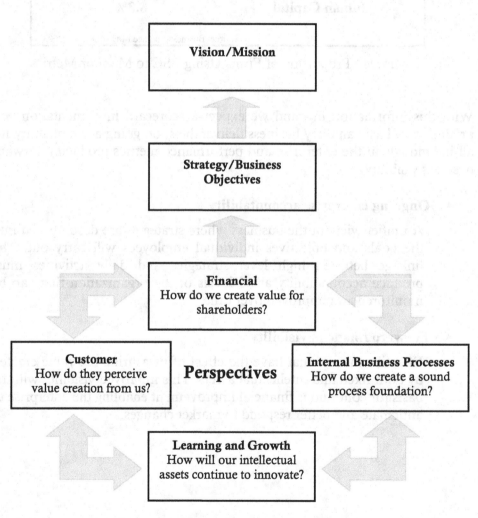

Source: Adapted from "The Strategy-Focused Organization", by Kaplan & Norton

Exhibit 5. Four Perspectives and Their Links to the Business Vision

Financial Perspective

How do we create value for our shareholders?

Accounting for the real cost of capital as well as knowing the true valuation of the enterprise's fixed and intangible assets will allow an accurate measurement of value creation. Existing financial systems lack sufficient leading indicators inhibiting the firm's ability to respond to the market and, therefore, diminishing its financial performance. A complete financial perspective by the firm will include the value of its intangible assets for an accurate valuation as well as sufficient leading indicators to create forward financial visibility. Further, the high performance organization will have valued its intangible assets to ascertain the true value of the firm.

Customer Perspective

How do our customers perceive value creation from us?

This perspective captures the ability of the organization to provide quality goods and services, effective delivery, and overall customer satisfaction, as a minimum. Extended requirements include the segmentation of the customer base to determine profitability of customers and service programs, branding initiatives, and more. Enhanced visibility into customer profitability will enable further investment where most appropriate likely having the effect of improving customer satisfaction. The high performance organization will find and continue to invest on those customer segments that are most profitable to start a virtuous cycle of high return investment focused on customer satisfaction.

Business Process Perspective

How do we create a sound business process foundation upon which we can enable optimum financial performance?

This perspective compares internal business results against measures that lead to financial success and satisfied customers. To meet financial objectives and customer expectations, organizations must identify and optimize the key business processes. Key processes must be monitored to ensure continuing improvement and adaptation of new technologies and best practices. Internal business processes provide a foundation upon which every other perspective can achieve optimum execution. The high performance organization will utilize its business processes as a platform for introducing innovation and new technologies that will sustain its competitive advantage.

Learning and Growth Perspective or Intellectual Asset Development
How will our intellectual assets ensure learning and growth?

This perspective captures the capability of employees, information systems, and organizational alignment to manage the business and adapt to change. The organization will succeed only if employees are adequately trained and motivated and supplied with effective tools and information. The various core competencies required for competitiveness will best be maintained and developed by a motivated and capable workforce.

The challenges of globalization place special requirements on organizational development whereby organizations are now expected to respond nimbly and quickly to market variables. Shortened product life cycles require organizations and individuals to continuously enhance learning and capabilities. Intellectual asset development and their value creation capability need to be considered, and accounted for, as investment by the organization.

The high performance organization will have anticipated industry trends and responded by retraining or changing the workforce to secure an advantage over competitors.

2.5 The Value Of Intangible Assets

We encounter the subject of intangible asset valuation when we address the financial perspective of a firm. Although we will address valuation of intangible assets in the next chapter, let us now preview a financial tool used in this area.

EVA

Economic Value Added (EVA), developed by Stern Stewart & Co., is the financial performance measure that attempts to capture the true economic profit of a firm by taking into account the cost of capital incurred by the enterprise assets. EVA provides an estimate of true economic profit, or the amount by which earnings exceed or miss the required minimum rate of return that shareholders could get by investing in other securities of comparable risk. In short, EVA is net operating profit after taxes (NOPAT) minus a charge for the opportunity cost of all capital invested in an enterprise.

The charge for the cost of capital is the most important element of EVA. Under conventional accounting, most companies appear profitable but many in fact are not. As Peter Drucker put the matter in a Harvard Business Review article, "Until a business returns a profit that is greater than its cost of capital, it operates at a loss. Never mind that it pays taxes as if it had a genuine profit. The enterprise still returns less to the economy than it devours in resources. Until then it does not create wealth; it destroys it." EVA corrects this error by explicitly recognizing that when managers employ capital they must pay for it, just as if it were a wage.

As expected, industry research shows the limitations of EVA, mostly dealing with lack of agreement about the cost of capital, the lack of official rules about implementing the method, and difficulties in setting performance targets. [9]

The high performance enterprise must find a way for extracting maximum value of all its tangible and non-tangible assets and incorporating that value into an accurate financial perspective. Industry has not mastered the art and science of producing an accurate company valuation. Consider a survey conducted by the Institute of Management Accountants (IMA) who found that more than 40 percent of respondents are in the process of changing their performance measurement systems. Of those, approximately 70 percent describe the change as a "major overhaul" or "replacement" of the old system. [IMA, 2002]. Judging from these results, much work remains to produce an accurate valuation of the firm.

Generally Accepted Accounting Principles (GAAP) are Insufficient to Measure Total Value of the Firm.

The difference between market capitalization of a company and its book value reflects the way traditional accounting looks at fixed assets. The problem is that this approach does not fully integrate the value of intangible assets into financial reports.

The high performance enterprise must identify the real issues that impact financial performance and lead to the creation of long-term shareholder returns. A way must be found to overcome the deficiencies of the GAAP to present a true valuation of the companies.

Intellectual capital, human capital and internal processes may account for a large part of the value of the modern enterprise but they are not accurately calculated. In the knowledge-based firm only purchased intellectual property is measured at cost. There exists little recognition for internally produced intellectual property.

Rather than looking at an asset only on the basis of market value or depreciated value, companies could determine contribution to profitability by assigning a relative financial value to those assets supporting intangible activities. Consider these mission-critical areas of the firm,

- Customers
- Suppliers
- Human Resources
- Inventory

about which improved metrics can help bridge the gap between market capitalization and book value. The new view will not necessarily be purely financial or operational, but it will contain elements of both. Certain factors in assigning value to assets are critical to this view:

- Profitability strategies
- Total Cost of Ownership (TCO) of the asset
- Impact of asset availability on revenue and profitability
- Contribution of the asset to strategic initiatives

This view can be used to implement business process efficiencies and reduce cost. It can also be used to establish the linkage of strategic objectives with supporting assets thereby improving visibility into financial performance of various strategic initiatives.

2.6 A Basic Approach For Implementing A Scorecard

The value we see in the BSC is that it attempts to produce the two requirements for achieving high business performance indicated earlier. First, ongoing accountability at all levels; that is, the stakeholders are fully aligned through their activities to the organization's strategy. And second, forward financial visibility through effective performance measurements.

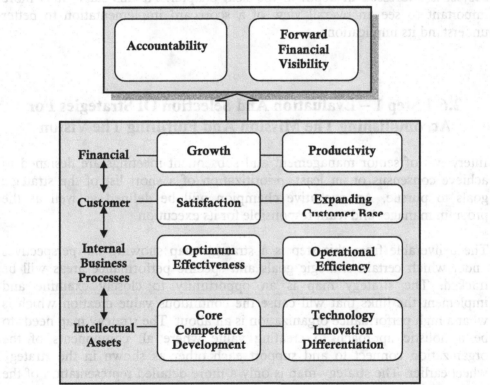

Source: Adapted from "The Strategy-focused Organization" by Kaplan & Norton

Exhibit.6. A Generic Strategy Map

The information technology (IT) infrastructure and investment required for a successful scorecard implementation varies with the size and complexity of the organization. It is not necessary to possess the specialized and latest BSC software tools available in the market. Most importantly, an effective implementation depends on the ability to discern the operational factors that impact financial performance, the experience and common sense to understand the human factors that facilitate or obstruct business processes, and the overall ability to understand cause and effect modalities in business operations. It must be clear that a scorecard will impact all major enterprise processes in a major way. In fact, the highest performance improvement will be extracted from Enterprise Resource Planning (ERP), Customer Relationship Management (CRM), Supply Chain Management (SCM), and Business Process Improvement (BPI).

The method presented here will not elaborate on performance metrics as this subject is addressed in depth in the next chapter. At this stage, it is more important to see an overall view of a scorecard implementation to better understand its implications.

2.6.1 Step 1 – Evaluation And Selection Of Strategies For Accomplishing The Mission And Fulfilling The Vision

Interviews of senior management and subsequent meetings are designed to achieve consensus or, at least, prioritization of a short list of the strategic goals to pursue. An executive champion will be defined as well as the program manager and team responsible for its execution.

The deliverable from this step is a strategy map showing the perspectives under which certain strategic goals and specific performance areas will be tracked. The strategy map is an opportunity to closely examine and implement the links that will cause the continuous value creation which is what a high performance organization is all about. The strategy map needs to be a holistic approach to creating value where all components of the organization connect to and support each other as shown in the strategy wheel earlier. The strategy map is only a more detailed representation of the strategy wheel where specific goals are identified and where intangible assets or investment can be linked to operational initiatives for valuation. A strategy map needs to reflect the organization's priorities and environment; it is not necessary to remain bound by Kaplan and Norton's four perspectives. In fact, the firm should review at this time the applicable perspectives to be used. In the example below, several strategic initiatives are shown,

Financial Goals	Customer Satisfaction
• Revenue Increase • Margins Increase • Cash Flow Velocity Increase	• Customer Profitability • Product Returns Reduction • Customer Base Increase
Business Processes Efficiency	Intellectual Assets
• Time to Market • Call Center • Accounts Receivable	• Intellectual Asset Revenue • Employee Development • Employee Productivity

Source: Recova Research

Exhibit 7. Strategy Map

2.6.2 Step 2 – Metrics Development

Metrics development will be addressed in Chapter 3, as part of Valuation of Assets. For now we will only describe suitable performance measurement associated with the scorecard methodology map we are developing.

In general, however, it is imperative to think of simplicity in terms of developing the right set of metrics that will track the progress and performance of strategic initiatives; the fewer the better. Past history is one criterion to use, where improvement over past performance can provide guidance. Another criterion could leverage new features or new information provided by the IT infrastructure. In any case, keep it simple. For example, performance metrics are shown below; these could be single or composite metrics:

Goals	*Performance Metrics*
Revenue Increase	Product Release Frequency
Margins Improvement	Customer Support Cost
Cash Flow Velocity	Cash-to-Cash Cycle Time
Customer Profitability	Revenue/Customer/Product Family
Time to Market Improvement	Product Development Cycle Time
Intellectual Asset Revenue	Patent/Licensing Revenue

Source: Recova Research

Exhibit 8. Goals and Suggested Performance Metrics

2.6.3 Step 3 – Implementation

At this stage, the following steps are necessary:

- **Identify owners and areas of responsibility for the various projects**

  Accountability requires that every participant understands and supports the contribution required for success.

- **Identify metrics owners**

  Some training may be necessary when dealing with new perspectives in terms of metrics or to accommodate IT infrastructure rigidities.

- **Set up reporting frequency and formats**

  Establishing the venue and format of these reports strengthens the value of a scorecard implementation and improves communication of the firm's strategy at all levels of the organization.

- **Identify required IT infrastructure**

  The complexity of IT support is determined by the complexity of the undertaking. Data warehouses, datamarts, software applications, and Intranet reporting capabilities need to be assessed for their relevance in supporting the scorecard implementation.

- **Design dashboard and familiarize participants with dashboard format and purpose**

  Beta tests and familiarization with the dashboard and mechanics of data acquisition and reporting should be conducted prior to startup. This is an opportunity to get employees involved in the actual "running" of the firm and they should be motivated accordingly.

The deliverable for a completed scorecard implementation should be a dashboard, or performance report showing the metrics discussed above in a simple and easy to use format. Industry provides ready-made dashboard products but, again, an internally developed report utilizing existing IT tools is often sufficient as an initial step. It is also necessary to consider outside help early on if complexity of a scorecard implementation is beyond internal skills.

A dashboard presents multidimensional views of performance data associated to the strategic initiatives and business goals of the enterprise.

The key success factor for a dashboard is the visualization of the actual and real time business performance of the firm at different levels of responsibility. The executive view will present performance summaries of key business areas whereas the analyst view will consist of more detailed metrics with multidimensional links to the information source. The dashboard should provide some basic features:

- Data drill down capability
- Time-based performance metrics
- High-Low limits where applicable
- Color coding for easy visualization
- Multidimensional data repositories

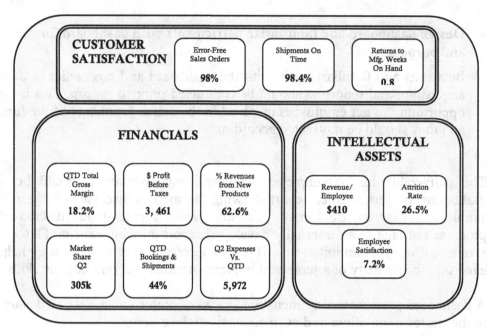

Source: Recova Research

Exhibit 9. Sample Dashboard

2.6.4 Step 4 – Continuous Adaptation

Completing the scorecard project enables the organization to impact the performance of the firm. Visualization of the parameters that affect performance is key in effecting improvement along the perspectives the firm considers relevant.

After the scorecard project is up and running, participants will usually start identifying improvements or corrections that become evident providing the opportunity to tap into the creativity and interest of many individuals.

A pitfall of similar projects is to view the scorecard as another administrative burden detracting from the task of actually "doing" things.

Benefits of a Scorecard Implementation

- Provides visibility into the firm's ongoing performance
- Provides tool for improved business performance
- Improves understanding and communication of the firm's business objectives
- Links the executive suite with employees to focus on common objectives

Pitfalls

- If mismanaged, it is perceived as additional administrative burden
- If poorly communicated, it becomes source of contention
- If poorly implemented, it prevents the firm from improving performance

---

By completing this chapter the reader has an improved understanding of the role that strategy definition and implementation plays in determining the business performance of the firm. Generic strategy maps and performance measurements as well as a simplified scorecard methodology have been presented to guide the reader in an actual scorecard implementation. The reader has also been exposed to the concept of valuation of intangible assets and how such a valuation can improve the actual measurement of a firm's performance.

References

[1] Cisco Systems, www.cisco.com, 2003

[2] D. Aaker, *Strategic Market Management*, 1998

[3] www.planware.org

[4] *The Economist*, December 2003

[5] Recova Research, 2003

[6] GartnerG2, Nov 30, 2001

[7] Cognos Inc., "80% fail because of the lack of a BI strategy", Oct 7, 2002

[8] Dr. M. Pohl, AST IT Consulting, South Africa

[9] *Quinnipiac University Report*, 2003

Chapter III
Measuring The Financial Value And Performance Of The Enterprise

In this chapter the reader will learn the criteria required for developing a performance metrics framework. Sample metrics are presented in the context of enterprise systems such as Customer Relationship Management (CRM), Supply Chain Management (SCM), and Enterprise Resource Management (ERP) whose valuation is useful to do when conducting a scorecard implementation or when conducting valuation of intangible assets.

You can't manage what you don't measure....

W.E. Demming

3.0 A Simple Criteria For Developing Metrics

If you can not manage what you do not measure, you certainly can not improve what you do not measure. Metrics need to be developed based on the key drivers that support the business strategy while processes must be designed to collect, track, and analyze them. In the end, the value of a metrics framework resides in its ability to transform data into information and knowledge that enables forward financial visibility and improved decision making. Leading indicators provide forward financial visibility that enables management to anticipate business trends.

It was clear from Chapter Two that developing a set of performance metrics that accurately measure enterprise performance will require a great deal of care and insight into the business. It is easy to create metrics that miss the mark. A set of simple measures that actually help in understanding the business requires thoughtful analysis and in-depth understanding of the business goals.

In general, Webster defines measure as "*The act or process of determining extent, dimensions, etc.; especially as determined by a standard.*" To better suit our purpose, we define performance metrics as measures indicating the degree of progress or achievement in reaching pre-established enterprise performance goals.

Software vendors offer a variety of canned packages dealing with scorecard metrics. From our experience, it is best for the practitioner to understand in detail how these metrics and measurement frameworks should be created before using automated tools. This enables optimum utilization of whatever tools are available. Some guidelines for creating a metrics framework are:

- The fewer metrics the better

- Every metric should be linked to a traditional financial measurement and should be unique in describing an activity

- The framework should provide metrics that relate to established standards, whenever possible

- The metrics should be measurements that can be readily derived or acquired from existing information systems

- Metrics should be presented as a management dashboard showing strategic feedback and performance trends

The Baldrige Criteria Booklet of 1997 puts it clearly… "*A major consideration in performance improvement involves the creation and use of performance measures or indicators. Performance measures or indicators are measurable characteristics of products, services, processes and operations the company uses to track and improve performance. The measures or indicators should be selected to best represent the factors that lead to improved customer, financial, and operational performance. A comprehensive set of measures and indicators tied to customer and/or company performance requirements represent a clear basis for aligning all activities with the company goals. Through the analysis of data from the tracking processes, the measures or indicators themselves may be evaluated and changed to better support such goals.*"

3.1 Segmentation Of Customer Base And Sample Customer Performance Measurements

The CIO.com newsletter, (June 11, 2003) reports, *"Bearing Point surveyed 167 companies, each with more than $1 billion in annual revenues, and found that while 82 percent of companies indicated that they view CRM as important, only 37 percent are achieving expected performance. For 2003, 26 percent of companies are forging ahead with their CRM investment but overall investment in CRM is down 30 percent year-over-year, according to the survey...."*

It is evident that these companies haven't clearly defined and linked the metrics for their Customer Relationship Management (CRM) projects to their customer strategy. Broken links result in a predictable loss of financial performance.

Additional industry polls reveal that four out of five IT managers must now demonstrate a ROI for major systems prior to their implementation. Clearly, a gap exists between strategic intent and actual results and a contributing factor is the lack of suitable measurement frameworks. All this means industry wastes billions of dollars through poor strategy execution.

In terms of devising a performance metrics framework consider two types of metrics; key performance indicators relating to financial variables (customer base segmentation) and those relating to effective use by employees of the available technology and systems (rate of increase of customer database entries, for example). The former evaluates how well the enterprise is received by customers and the latter how well the firm is positioning itself for growth and increased revenue.

The customer dimension is a prime candidate for reviewing well-defined metrics. In general, a simple table can be useful in visualizing strategic initiatives and their associated metrics or measurements. A sample follows:

GOALS	MEASURES
Improve Customer Satisfaction	• Price Relative to Competition • Delivery Time, Lead Time • Product Reliability • Ease of Use • Purchasing Experience • Support Rating • Market Share • Customer Acquisition • Customer Buying Pattern • Customer Segment Improvement

Exhibit 1. Measures for Improving Customer Satisfaction

Understanding the composition of the customer base in terms of profitability to the business is extremely useful. This segmentation could be achieved through data mining the customer database. Using this information one may segment the customer base into a typology such as loyal and switchable types, for example. In determining customer profitability the following measures could be used:

GOALS	MEASURES
Improve Customer Profitability	• Product Cost • Order Cost • Selling Cost • Transportation Cost • Application Cost • Design Engineering Cost • Presale Cost • Production Cost • Distribution Cost • Support Cost • Customer Profit Contribution

Exhibit 2. Measures for Improving Customer Profit Contribution

When these measures are known, they can be compared against realized revenue to show profitability of customer types. Customer types are defined as:

- **High-Profit Customers**

Customers who generate significant profit contributions are rarely defined by a single demographic group or region; therefore, they can be difficult to pre-identify, particularly in the embryonic stages of a market life cycle. A customer base financial analysis is necessary to discover the potential financial gain.

A customer-base analysis can reveal the quantities customers purchase and how much it costs to serve them. A robust cost-accounting system can reveal data by product, order, and account, and can capture costs beyond the factory, including selling, transportation, application engineering, design engineering and post-sale servicing.

When these costs are known by account, the firm can plot them against realized prices to show the dispersion of the account profitability. Recognizing high contribution customers allows the firm to focus on acquiring and defending their most profitable accounts. Changes in the firm's value proposition, competitive pressures, and transitions into more mature market phases can translate into significant shifts of customer profitability. Continuing analysis of accounts in this category is therefore recommended.

As an example, an electronic materials supplier was investing its marketing resources equally in three different customer groups: original equipment manufacturers (OEMs), large independents, and small custom-fabrication shops. When an in-depth customer base analysis was completed, several things became clear with respect to customer profitability. The large OEMs were generating 35% operating margins, while the small custom-fabrication shops were generating 15% operating losses. The large OEM customers, even though fewer in number, were highly profitable because of low-price sensitivity and low-service requirements. The company realized that it was under-investing in the OEM customers and was beginning to lose them to a smaller competitor that was funneling all its resources toward acquiring them. Eventually the company re-channeled its marketing investment to defend and re-acquire the OEM accounts and, in the process, acquired several new high-profit OEM customers. [1]

- **Share-Determining Customers**

Certain customers act as "early adopters" in markets and thereby influence the purchasing patterns of followers. This secondary effect on market share can heavily influence a firm's long-term strategic position. Since little customer support might exist in the growth phases of a market cycle and a supplier's resources might be extended by the overall growth in demand, a disciplined commitment to acquire these key customers is required. In return, these accounts can deliver higher returns than other types because of their influence in the market place.

One way to identify share-determining customers is that they typically grow notably faster than the industry averages. Some share-determining targets include key professional groups who represent buyers and organizations that create industry standards. Other customers control marketing channels and assist in validating the utility of a firm's products to the marketplace.

Assemblers, in many market situations, have sufficient influence over suppliers to qualify as a share-determining segment. In industrial software, for instance, major assemblers like Boeing and Ford can help determine suppliers' choices of systems. They can encourage or even mandate standardization to conform to the assembler's approach. [2]

- **Switchable and Loyal Customers**

In a maturing market, allegiance between suppliers and customers becomes an important factor. Switching costs often increase, particularly when non-interchangeable solutions compete for market share. Opportunities to attract customers can be created when a differential in service performance exists or when there is a mismatch between customer needs and supplier offerings.

Instability in the operating or financial performance by a competitor creates an opportunity for attracting customers. Depending on market characteristics, it may be important to differentiate between customers who always like to pursue the cheapest supplier (chronic switchers) and customers who are genuinely looking into switching to another source because they are legitimately unhappy with their current situation. Chronic Switchers can be exploited to satisfy unused capacity when marginal profits associated with acquisition exceed the marginal costs of serving them. Certainly, these are not strategic customers.

Customer types are shown in the following diagram, in terms of an arbitrary distribution. We expect an actual segmentation would be developed through analysis of market intelligence acquired by the firm.

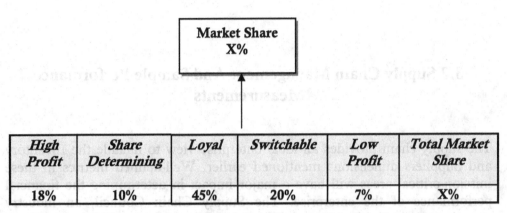

High Profit	Share Determining	Loyal	Switchable	Low Profit	Total Market Share
18%	10%	45%	20%	7%	X%

Exhibit 3. Segmentation of Customer Base by Profit Types

An investment factor, based on business imperatives, could be associated with this segmentation to prioritize investment that would expand the customer base or focus on higher revenue support contracts, for example;

Customer Type

	High Profit	Share Determining	Loyal	Switchable	Low Profit	Total
	18%	10%	45%	20%	7%	X%
Investment Factor	5	4	3	2	1	
Score	0.9	0.4	1.35	0.4	0.01	

Exhibit 4. Segmentation of Customer Base and Investment Factors

In this example, investment priority should be given to the loyal segment where the majority, 45% of customers, resides in order to capture the largest revenue. This kind of visibility allows management to consider investment options designed to change the composition of the customer base, if that matches a strategic direction for the business. In addition, the relevant assets can be linked indirectly through accounts receivables, to the customer types (High profit, low profit) that they serve.

3.2 Supply Chain Management And Sample Performance Measurements

The supply chain provides an ideal enterprise view to include the Inventory and Suppliers dimensions mentioned earlier. Well-defined metrics in these mission-critical areas will have a major impact in determining the financial performance of the enterprise. The Supply Chain Council, an industry organization, is creating a standards-based metrics framework. Through these efforts, the Supply Chain Operations Reference model (SCOR) offers an industry standard for supply chain improvement, including metrics. Some of these metrics are reflected below.

Achieving supply chain excellence brings about increased competitiveness. Some benefits are:

- Improved agility in responding to markets shifts
- Reduced costs in dealing with suppliers and distributors
- Improved build-to-order capability
- Efficient and effective order fulfillment process
- Improved quality and manufacturing efficiencies

Some of the immediate business goals benefiting from those benefits may include:

- Increasing ROA across the supply chain by sharing inventory responsibility
- Increasing velocity of replenishment and time to market for new products
- Reducing supply and supplier vulnerability (time delays, variable quality)
- Reducing the cost of capital by optimizing the cash-to-cash cycle

As in the customer segmentation example, measuring the cash flow contribution of each customer allows us to align enterprise assets to customers and business processes in order to optimize shareholder return. A Cash Velocity measurement is especially useful when evaluating financial performance of the Supply Chain. Factors affecting cash velocity are inventory turnover, transaction costs, average collection time, and others. The Cash-to-Cash metric is designed to measure cash velocity as a way to produce positive cash flows.

Reducing the cost of capital by optimizing the cash-to-cash cycle time can be facilitated by expediting receivables collection. Cash-to-cash cycle time is a composite metric describing the average days required to transform a dollar invested in raw materials into a dollar collected from a customer. Encouraging electronic funds transfers though discounts, for example, would be an effective mechanism for rapid payment.

Pittiglio Rabin Todd & McGrath, a research company, found that by using the SCOR benchmarks, best-in-class companies showed significantly better supply-chain performance over competitors. For example, they filled 95% of orders from inventory, compared with a high-tech industry median of 86%, and improved annual inventory turns from a median of 2.4 turns per year to 6.9 turns. These improvements have a direct impact on companies' bottom lines. Cash-to-cash cycle times averaged 28 days for top performers, vs. a 71-day median. And top performers were able to improve delivery performance while reducing their average time holding inventory to 29 days, vs. an industry median of 64 days. [1]

Let's discuss the components of a supply chain in terms of a metrics framework:

- Planning
    Defining the supply chain strategy for the firm decomposed into business goals. A metrics framework should be defined at this stage to track the effectiveness of the supply chain overall and business goals in particular.

- Sourcing
    Selecting suppliers that deliver inputs required in producing the firm's products or services. A specific business objective here would be to reduce supply and supplier variability and the relevant metrics would

track the effectiveness of vendor processes such as inventory, receiving inspections, product returns, and payments.

- Making

    Manufacturing the product or executing the service. Metrics here would tend to monitor operational cost-effectiveness, cycle times, and cost of capital.

- Delivering

    Making the product or service available to the customer. Emphasis here would be placed on cost and speed.

- Returning

    The processes designed to receive defective products from customers, resolve product problems, and reimburse the value of product. Metrics here should be designed to understand the underlying quality issues as well as the total cost of returns to the firm.

A well-designed metrics framework would help the high performance enterprise to optimize the business processes contained by every supply chain component. The complex interactions caused by internal and external linkages to suppliers, partners, and customers require continuing business process improvements. Distribution models related to the supply chain benefit immediately from process analysis and improvement as inefficiencies, bottlenecks, and duplication are quickly identified and corrected. These dollars directly affect the bottom line.

Several Supply Chain valuation methods are available to the readers seeking improved financial visibility:

- **ROI (Return on Investment)**

    Calculates the total return on specific investments and the time necessary to recover that investment.

- **ROA (Return on Assets)**

    Factors velocity and profit margin providing a good indication of the degree of financial performance.

- **Cash-to-Cash Cycle Time**
  Measures the ability to generate positive cash turns.

- **EVA (Economic Value Added)**
  Measures the return of investment in terms of cost of capital.

Enhanced visibility in the performance of the Supply Chain directly facilitates the formulation of competitive strategies for the enterprise. Competitive positioning requires in-depth understanding of distribution channels, differentiation factors, and the overall value proposition. We need now to think in terms of Value Chain valuation.

Value chains deal with internal and external integration, collaboration and synchronization. Internally we try to integrate the supply chain functions and assets across the enterprise. Externally we collaborate with suppliers, customers, and freight forwarders. Overall, we try to synchronize and optimize the supply chain functions across all boundaries to create value for the stakeholders.

Several valuation methods need to be considered: [2]

- **Internal Cost Analysis**
  Determines the sources of profitability and the relative cost impact of internal value-creating assets and processes.

- **Internal Differentiation Analysis**
  Determines the sources of differentiation, including the cost, within internal value-creating assets and processes.

- **Extended Linkage Analysis**
  Determines the relationships and associated costs among suppliers, partners, and customers in order to maximize the value delivered to customers and to minimize cost.

The resulting set of analyses can be organized around three frameworks [3]:

- **Industry Structure Analysis**
  The profitability of an industry as measured by the long-term ROI of the average company.

- **Core Competency Analysis**
  The intellectual capital valuation of core competencies. (See section 3.3 on Valuation of Intellectual Capital)

- **Segmentation Analysis**
  Industry segmentation, similar to the CRM segmentation shown earlier, can shed light on the competitive landscape and facilitate the formulation of strategies for the firm.

All these analyses leading to formulation of competitive strategies start with well-defined measurements frameworks that provide the necessary information. The following tables show sample measurements associated with goals or strategic initiatives designed to improve efficiencies throughout the supply chain.

Goals	*Measurements*
Planning Efficiency Improvement	• Forecasting • Demand Management • Master Scheduling • Inventory Management • Business Planning • Capacity Planning • Distribution Planning • Channel Sell-Through Analysis

Exhibit 5. Categories to Measure Efficiency Improvements

Goals	*Measurements*
Production Cost Reduction	• Labor Cost • Materials Management • Production Planning • Receiving Inspection • Material Conversion • Repair, Rebuild, Recycling, Disposal • Environmental Management

Exhibit 6. Measurements for Reducing Production Costs

Goals	*Measurements*
Order Management Improvement	• Order Creation/Capture • Order Scheduling • Order Maintenance • Shipment Management • Customer Billing • Quotes • Perfect Order Factor (order entry accuracy, delivery on time, shipped with no damage, invoiced correctly) • Back Order • Customer Order Cycle Time • Customer Order Actual Time • On Time Delivery • Order Entry to Manufacturing Start • Start Manufacturing to Order Complete • Order Complete Manufacturing to Customer Receipt

Exhibit 7. Measurements for Improving Order Management

Goals	Measurements
Sourcing Efficiency Improvement	• Make vs. Buy Analysis • Supplier Relations Management • Procurement

Exhibit 8. Categories for Improving Sourcing Efficiency

Goals	Measurements

Distribution Improvement	• Transportation Management
	• Freight Cost Per Unit Shipped
	• Outbound Freight Costs as Percentage of Net Sales
	• Inbound Freight Costs as Percentage of Purchases
	• Transit Time
	• Claims as % of Freight Costs
	• Freight Bill Accuracy
	• Percent of Truckload Capacity Utilization
	• Truck Turnaround Time
	• Shipment Visibility/Traceability Percentage
	• On-time Pickups
	• Customer Shelf Replenishment
	• Delivery Management
	• Order Consolidation
	• Kitting, Packing, Shipping
	• Installation Cost
	• Returned Goods Management
	• Returns Processing Cost as %
	    ➤ Product Revenue
	    ➤ Returns Inventory
	    ➤ Returns Cycle Time
	    ➤ Cycle Time Returns Repairs

Exhibit 9. Measurements for Distribution Improvement

Goals	Measurements
Customer Accounting Cost Reduction	• Accounts Receivable Collection • Returns and Credits Management

Exhibit 10. Measurements for Reducing Accounting Costs

Goals	Measurements
Product Life Cycle (PLC) Cost Reduction	• New Product Data Management • Ramp-up Costs • End-of-Life Management • Cycle Time to Process Obsolete Product for Disposition • New Product Introduction Costs

Exhibit 11. Measurements for Reducing PLC Costs

Goals	Measurements
Administration Efficiency Improvements	• Import/Export Management • Supply Chain Financial Planning • Supply Chain IT • Performance Measurements

Exhibit 12. Categories for Measuring Efficiency Improvements

3.3 Intellectual Capital Investment
Developing A Measurements Framework For Quantifying
Intellectual Capital Value

The migration of manufacturing from America to the rest of the world in the 70s is evident again in 2003. The newly coined term "off-shoring" refers to the migration of the service sector jobs including software development and chip design to India, China and other countries. A recent article by Steven Greenhouse of the New York Times indicates "Forrester Research, a high-technology consulting group, estimates the number of service sector jobs newly located overseas...will climb to 3.3 million in 2015 from about 400,000 this year. This shift represents about 2% of all American jobs" [4]. The root cause for this new job migration is lower production costs and globalization imperatives.

Competitiveness dictates that a new advantage should be created when an industrial sector moves out. Particularly applicable to America, innovation could be that competitive advantage. Richard O. Hundley, lead author of a study by the Rand's National Defense Research Institute indicates that the United States would continue to "lead the information technology revolution for years to come because American businesses are focused on innovation..." [5]

For this to be true, it necessitates that a firm's most valuable asset, intellectual capital and its human resources, be measured with objective metrics that associate their tangible value with strategic objectives. Business journals report that in today's U.S. economy, 80 percent of gross domestic product and private non-farm employment is in the services sector, where much of the output is knowledge-based. The cost components of today's products consist mostly of R&D, intellectual assets, and services.

Valuing intangible assets is an art and a science well beyond the scope of this brief guide. Our emphasis is on presenting our research on measurements that the reader might find readily useful. We will, however, mention some of the Valuation methods presently available.

Book to Market Value

The difference between book value and market value represents the value of intellectual capital of the firm. As indicated previously, the flaw in this method is that book value measures fixed assets while the market measures the entire firm. The book to market value calculation ignores factors that influence investor's perception of income generation potential, such as intellectual capital and other intangible assets.

Tobin's Q

A ratio named after Nobel Economics Laureate James Tobin of Yale University. He hypothesized that the combined market value of all companies on the stock market should be equal to their replacement cost. Q is the ratio of the market value of a firm's assets divided by their replacement value.

Relative Value

Bob Buckman (Buckman Laboratories) and Leif Edvinsson (Skandia Insurance) are proponents of this approach, in which progress, not a quantitative target, is the ultimate goal. Example: have 80% of employees involved with the customer in some meaningful way.

Competency Models

By observing and classifying the behaviors of "successful" employees ("competency models") and calculating the market value of their output, it is possible to assign a dollar value to the intellectual capital they create and use in their work.

Subsystem Performance

Sometimes it is relatively easy to quantify success or progress in one intellectual capital component. For example, Dow Chemical was able to measure an increase in licensing revenues from better control of its patent assets.

Benchmarking

Involves identifying companies that are recognized leaders in leveraging their intellectual assets, determining how well they score on relevant criteria, and then comparing your own company's performance against that of the leaders. Example of a relevant criterion: leaders systematically identify knowledge gaps and use well-defined processes to close them.

Business Worth

This approach centers on three questions. What would happen if the information we now use disappeared altogether? What would happen if we doubled the amount of key information available? How does the value of this information change after a day, a week, and a year? Evaluation focuses on the cost of missing or under-utilizing a business opportunity, avoiding or minimizing a threat.

Business Process Auditing

Measures how information enhances value in a given business process, such as accounting, production, marketing, or purchasing.

Knowledge Bank

Treats capital spending as an expense (instead of an asset) and treats a portion of salaries (normally 100% expense) as an asset, since it creates future cash flows.

Brand Equity Valuation

Methodology that measures the economic impact of a brand (or other intangible asset) on such things as pricing power, distribution reach, ability to launch new products as "line extensions."

Calculated Intangible Value

Compares a company's return on assets (ROA) with a published average ROA for the industry.

Microlending

A new type of lending that substitutes intangible "collateral" (peer group support, training, and the personal qualities of entrepreneurs) for tangible assets. Primarily used to spur economic development in poor areas.

Colorized Reporting

Suggested by SEC commissioner Steven Wallman, this method supplements traditional financial statements (which give a "black and white" picture) with additional information (which adds "color"). Examples of "color" include Brand values, customer satisfaction measures, and value of a trained work force.

3.3.1 Intellectual Capital Components

Intellectual capital includes people's knowledge, skills, experience, and information. Depending on the environment, it could be categorized further as follows:

- **Intellectual Assets**
  - Patents
  - Trade marks
  - Copyrights

- **Knowledge Assets**
  - Customer data
  - Core competencies
  - Skills and experience
  - Human potential

- **Intangible Assets**
  - Brand names
  - Reputation
  - Customer relationship

In order to measure intellectual capital, a variety of quantitative metrics are proposed. They include skills assessments, performance rankings excluding forced ratings, income per employee, market value per employee, customer satisfaction indices, training costs and employee turnover rates. The application of knowledge creates business assets that can be quantified, such as customer buying patterns, relationships with customers and suppliers, the application of best practices, and new research initiatives, for example.

In addition to the Balanced Scorecard and EVA that are discussed elsewhere in this Guide, other measurements frameworks have come to our attention. We will discuss them briefly and construct metrics frameworks.

Intangible Asset Monitor (IAM)

Developed in 1987 by Karl-Erik Svibey. The IAM matrix identifies 3 types of intangible assets that could account for the Book to Market discrepancy. These are; Individual Competence (Education, skills, experience), Internal Structure (culture, internal processes) and External Structures (relationships with customers, firm's reputation). The other dimension deals with efficiency (getting the most from employees), stability (revenue predictability), and growth as well as renewal (innovation). A sample measurement framework is shown below:

	External Structure	*Internal Structure*	*Competence*
Efficiency	•Satisfied customer index •Sales/customer •Win/loss index	•Values/attitudes index •Percent support staff	•Percent professional •Value added/employee •Value added/professional •Profit/employee •Profit/professional
Stability	•Big customer ratio •Age structure •Devoted customer ratio •Frequency repeat orders	•Investment in IT •Structure enhancing customer	•Relative pay •Seniority •Professional turnover
Growth and Renewal	•Profit/customer •Image-enhancing customer •Organic growth	•Age of organization •Support staff turnover •Rookie Ratio •Seniority	•Educational level •Number years in profession •Training cost •Competence-enhancing customer

Exhibit 13. Intangible Asset Monitor Matrix and Measurements

Skandia Navigator

Skandia Navigator was developed by the Swedish financial services company. It focuses on:

- Financial (Lagging indicator)
- Process (Present indicator)
- Human (Present indicator)
- Customer (Present indicator)
- Renewal and development (Future indicator)

A matrix similar to the IAM could be developed by the reader to quantify these dimensions.

Intellectual Capital Index

The index created by Intellectual Capital Services, a research organization, identifies three categories:

- Human capital dealing with knowledge competence, experience, skills

- Structural capital dealing with business processes, information systems, databases

- Customer capital dealing with relationships, brands, reputation

The specific environment should help define the categories applicable to the enterprise. Emphasis should be placed on flows as well as the stocks of intellectual capital. With this in mind practitioners create an IC index and link it to market value of the enterprise. A sample measurement framework along the dimension of human, structural, and customer capital is shown below:

	Key Components	*Metrics*
Relationships, Brands, Reputation	Customers, Suppliers, Alliances, Partners, Stakeholders	• Length of Relationships • Customer Retention • Satisfaction Index • Customer Segmentation Metrics

Exhibit 14. Intellectual Capital Index – Customer Capital

	Key Components	*Metrics*
Organization	Infrastructure, Processes, Culture	• Revenue from Patents • Cycle Times • Process Times • Admin Cost/Revenue
Renewal and Development	New Output Development, Restructuring, R&D	• Percent Revenue from New Output • IT Literacy • Training Cost/Employee • New Patents Filed

Exhibit 15. Intellectual Capital Index – Structural Capital

	Key Components	*Metrics*
Competence	Knowledge, Skills, Talents, Experience	• Average Years of Service With Company • Number of Employees • Number of Managers • Revenue/Employee • Employee Turnover • Profits/Employee • Average Employee Age • Number Exempt Employees • Number of Full Time Employees • Number of Temporary Employees • Percent Company Managers With Advanced Degrees
Attitude	Motivation, Behavior, Conduct	• Leadership Index • Motivation Index • Hours Explaining
Intellectual Agility	Innovation, Imitation, Adaptation, Packaging	• Savings from Suggestions • Diversity Index • The Number of New Colleague to Colleague Relationships Spawned

	Key Components	Metrics
Intellectual Agility (continued)		(promote exchange of tacit knowledge) • The Reuse Rate of "Frequently Accessed" Knowledge • The Capture of Key Expertise Online • The Dissemination of Knowledge Sharing • Number of Knowledge Sharing Proficiencies Gained • The Number of New Ideas Generating Innovative Products or Services • The Number of Lessons Learned and Best Practices Applied to Create Value-added • The Number of Articles/Books Written • The Number of Talks at Conferences • Professional Development Investment • The Number of Apprentices Under Mentoring and Success of Apprentices • Interactions With Academicians/Consultants

Exhibit 16. Intellectual Capital Index- Human Capital

No methodology readily translates intangible assets into financial reports that account for the difference in market value versus book value. They do provide, however, an indication of the company's ability to turn intangible assets into financial capital.

A firm needs to identify the output indicators that best reflect the success factors critical to its business strategy. The quality of the indicators is reflected in their relevance and flexibility. They should also be cost-effective to collect and process, easily recorded, and able to be modified as needed.

3.4 Valuation of Intellectual Assets (IA)

We have presented, so far, asset performance metrics as well as a methodology for developing a performance measurement framework. The question now is; how do we actually transform an intangible asset into a dollar value and integrate these dollars into the existing system?

Research allows us to present a summary and examples of how this process is conducted. We must emphasize this is a very specialized and complex discipline and readers are encouraged to seek professional advice when dealing with these types of valuations.

Seeking a financial valuation of intellectual property is triggered by a variety of reasons, among them:

- Corporate mergers
- Management buy-outs
- Privatization of public assets
- Sale or licensing of specific intellectual assets (patents)
- Investment

Prior to valuation, an intangible asset should meet criteria, such as:

- Needs to be clearly identified and separable from other assets
- Needs to be aligned to present and future revenue
- Needs to be protected (patents, copyrights)
- Needs to be transferable

Valuation methods must be transparent, consistent, and verifiable. Some methods available to industry are:

- Market Value of firm less the Net Tangible Assets
- Cost-based (Historical and Replacement cost)
- Comparable Market Valuations
- Interbrand Survey

Market Value of Firm Less the Net Tangible Assets

This approach can be used to value intellectual capital assets (IA) of public companies where,

$$\text{Net Tangible Assets (N)} = \text{Total Assets (A)} - \text{Total Liabilities (L)}$$

Need to subtract any intangible assets (I) with book value

$$\text{Net Tangible Assets (N)} = A - L - I$$

Estimate Goodwill (G) at a standard 10% of capitalization (C) so that

$$C = N + G + IA, \text{ therefore}$$

$$IA = C (N + G) \text{ or } IA = 0.9C - N$$

The value of intellectual capital assets is, in fact, the residual value of the company after deducting the value of tangible assets and Goodwill. The weakness in this approach is that intellectual assets are not valued individually. The market, however, recognizes the value of intellectual assets and their potential for creating future value by valuing the firm above its book value.

Cost-based (Historical cost and Replacement cost)

The historical cost (H) is the actual cost incurred in creating and developing intellectual property assets. For instance, consider intellectual assets in the R&D phase, where researchers spent $100,000 per year for a project total of $200,000 (F). If cost of money (T) is 7% per year and if no premium is factored in for technical risk;

$$H = F + T = \$200,000 + [(100,000x7\%) + \$200,000x7\%)]$$

$$H = \$221,000$$

One of the problems with this approach is that there is no direct correlation between expenditure on a particular intellectual asset and its subsequent revenue potential. It provides, however, the minimum return needed to justify investment on an intellectual asset.

Replacement Cost Method

Replacement cost valuation (R) is based upon an assessment of the cost to replace the intellectual asset or to develop an alternate one. To carry out the valuation, an estimate is made of the time and resources necessary to develop a similar asset. Risk is also factored in (RP). Taking the previous R&D example:

$$R = (F + T) \times RP$$

where the chance of failure is 40%

$$RP = 100 / (100-40) = 1.67 \text{ , then}$$

$$R = (221,000) \times 1.67 = \$369,070$$

The investor could also think of this as the minimum return necessary on the R&D investment.

Comparable Market Valuations

For comparable market valuations to be valid there must be an active market that is trading in comparable assets. Several research organizations have gathered data for license royalty rates that could be used for comparative valuations of intellectual capital assets and for setting royalty rates.

A royalty stream is a measure of the value that an intellectual capital asset adds to a product or process over a product that is not protected by intellectual property rights. Thus, the present value (PV) for the royalty income equals the value of the asset.

An existing arbitrary rule of 25% exists whereby the licensor receives 25% of the profit from the branded or patented product. The licensee receives 75% to compensate for the risk and effort in final product development.

The Interbrand Survey

The Interbrand Survey published by Business Week magazine shows brand values of leading corporations and provides insight on valuation methodology [6]. The survey includes the following market capitalization and brand value for the following companies,

Firm	Market Capitalization, July 2001	Brand Value as Percent of Market Capitalization
Coca Cola	$113,000 m	61.00%
Microsoft	$380,000 m	17.00%
GE	$498,600 m	9.00%

Exhibit 17. Brand Value as Percent of Market Capitalization

The wide distribution of brand value among these firms is indicative of the complex variables underlying brand valuation. In valuing brands, Interbrand looks at four areas: [7]

- **Financial Forecasting**

  Starts with a projection of all revenues generated by the brand less all operating costs, corporation taxes, and a charge for the capital employed to operate the branded business. The result is Intangible Earnings representing all earnings generated by the intangibles of the branded business. The concept of Intangible Earnings is similar to value based profit models such as EVA, discussed earlier in this guide.

- **Role of Branding**

  Role of Branding analysis determines Brand Earnings as the percent of Intangible Earnings that are attributable solely to the brand. It identifies and weighs the key drivers of customer demand and their dependence on brands. This is calculated as a percentage and applied to Intangible Earnings to derive Brand Earnings.

- **Brand Risk**

  Brand Risk analysis provides the specific risk rate at which the forecasted Brand Earnings are discounted to their Net Present Value. The analysis assesses the risk profile of the projected Brand Earning based on the security of the brand franchise.

- **Brand Value Calculation**

  Value of the brands has been calculated as the net present value of the projected Brand Earnings. The value of the brand depends both on a good financial performance and a strong marketing position. Sometimes even if short-term earnings performance is weakened, investment in the brand can produce better long term results, a stronger brand, and consequently, a higher Brand Value.

Recognition of the economic value of brands has increased the demand on the management of the brand as another intangible asset. Essential to extracting value from brand management is the need to align it with value-based management systems such as EEVA, EVA, and well-designed metrics frameworks, as presented earlier in this guide.

- **Economic Benefits Valuation**

  Is based upon the principle that an intellectual capital asset must produce a net economic benefit during its lifetime in order to have a value. During the R&D phase, for example, a project and associated intellectual capital asset are a liability since capital is being consumed and income generally is not being produced. To account for this variable generation of income we need to consider Life Cycle Costing, Net Present Value (NPV) and Discounted Cash Flow (DCF).

To arrive at the present value of a new intellectual capital asset, it is necessary to calculate:

- The net cost of design, research, development, production, marketing, and distribution.
- The life of the product or process
- The life of the associated intellectual capital asset
- The timing and extent of the income stream

For an intellectual capital asset already generating an income a DCF method will suffice. This also leads to the NPV of the asset.

The reader has now been exposed in some depth to the intricacies of developing performance metrics for the enterprise. This overview would be helpful in a scorecard implementation or when conducting valuation of intellectual or intangible enterprise assets. In reading this and the previous chapters the reader is equipped now to apply this or a similar methodology when attempting to visualize the firm's level of performance.

References

[1], [2] Andrian J. Slywotzky and Benson P. Shapiro, " Leveraging to Beat the Odds: The New Market Mind – Set", *Harvard Business Review*, September-October 1993.

[3] *Optimizing Magazine*, December 2001

[4], [5] The American Institute of Certified Public Accountants (AICPA), 1998

[6], [7] *Business Week Magazine*, August 6, 2001

CHAPTER IV
A Continuous Adaptation Methodology And New Financial Concepts, Extended Capital Management (ECM) And Extended EVA (EEVA)

In this chapter the reader will explore a continuous adaptation methodology leading to ever higher levels of business performance in response to changes in the firm's environment. This methodology will be based on on-going evaluation of business processes, of existing targets and goals, and of strategy alignment. The reader will also become familiar with new concepts in financial management that offer insight in revealing the true value and profitability of the firm.

> ## "Only the paranoid survive"
> ### - Andy Grove

4.1 A Continuous Adaptation Methodology

The challenges of competition require a firm to never stand still; "...only the paranoid survive..." according to Andy Grove of Intel Semiconductors. Once the firm achieves a certain level of success, competitors will actively work to imitate and remove that advantage.

The high performance firm will always remain adaptable to internal and external changes that affect its ability to perform. These changes can take many forms; from currency valuation to technology obsolescence to political unrest, and many more. Short product life cycles are becoming increasingly common in this age of globalized competition while the process of outsourcing and offshoring manufacturing services and software development add uncertainty to labor markets around the world.

The table below summarizes a past and future view regarding changes in our environment. The future view shows increasing complexity as well as the need to optimize quality and utilization of intellectual assets. Clearly, an approach consisting of continuous adaptation to its environment is required to formalize the firm's process of innovation and performance improvement.

ENVIRONMENT	PAST	FUTURE	REASON
Business Predictability	Predictable	Unpredictable	Fast changes in technology
Customer Profile	Mass Marketing	Ultra-diversified	Ability to understand individual preferences
Employee Skills	Low	High	Job complexity
Management Style	Directive	Leading	Higher recognition of employee contribution
Management System	Results-oriented	Results and process oriented	Higher recognition of quality content

Exhibit 1. Factors Affecting Changes in Business Environment

Most factors affecting the business environment are outside our control. It is imperative then to adopt a response that provides a clear view of where the firm has been and where it needs to be to retain or improve its competitive advantage. In general our approach to achieve the next level of performance will result in

- **Anticipating change and issues**
  A great deal of operational efficiency can be achieved through root cause analysis. As our ability to understand business processes increases so does our ability to conduct scenario-based planning that help anticipate situations and outcomes. This forward-looking capability is key in generating organized change and reducing uncertainty.

- **Improving the customer interface**
  Previous chapters in this guide have shown it is possible to gain a very detailed understanding of customer behavior. Business intelligence tools and methods can help gain knowledge of individual customer

behavior. This increased knowledge presents an opportunity to achieve true customer intimacy and the potential to increase market share.

- **Improving intellectual assets**
  A most productive enterprise asset is a motivated and trained workforce. Employees taking responsibility for improving their contribution and their own capabilities ensure strategy and execution are correctly linked. Improved intellectual assets can also translate into additional sources of revenue for the firm.

- **Improving forward financial visibility**
  As discussed in Chapter 3, improving forward financial visibility enables management to produce a better and quicker response to changes in the marketplace. The ability to respond faster than the competition plays a key role in ensuring competitiveness.

A firm's current level of performance versus desirable states is shown in Exhibit 2. Leveraging from A. H. Maslow's hierarchy description of needs for individuals, we can develop a similar hierarchical view applicable to a firm's performance.

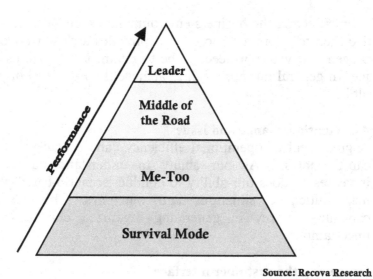

Source: Recova Research

Exhibit 2. Hierarchical Performance Progression for Enterprises

At the bottom level of business performance, the *Survival Mode*, a firm struggles to conduct business with questionable mid-term survival prospects. At this stage business models are weak and capitalization is difficult to obtain revenue. Revenue is based on low margin products or services, competitors inhibit growth, and there are few possibilities of being acquired by a larger company. Some restaurants and small service providers tend to belong to this sector, hence their low survival rates.

The *Me-Too* firms show little differentiation from their competitors. They are able to cover their operational cost but are mostly unable to invest in their future. Revenue is based on low margin products. Their product offering may be aging and their lack of capitalization diminishes their survival possibilities. They may however possess a respectable market share or brand name that might be the source of interest from larger companies interested in an acquisition.

The *Middle of the Road* performers can invest in their future. Their technical or service offering is attractive enough to drive strategic partnerships and to attract investment. They can hold their own in their market space through reasonably frequent new product rollouts and some innovation. They may have a niche in certain high end products and may claim some branding reputation.

The *Leaders* are clearly in control of their future. They consistently beat the competition in new product rollouts and they exhibit a clear technological edge that translates into high quality revenue. They are able to erect barriers of competition and grow aggressively. Their business model is sound, innovation-friendly, and able to withstand abrupt market changes. These are the companies that invest during an economic recession. Cisco Systems would belong in this performance space

4.2 Four Steps For Continuous Adaptation

Wherever a firm is in the hierarchy of performance needs there is no guarantee they may remain there. All firms, in order to maintain or improve their performance standing must continually examine their business model, their competitive standing in their industry, and their ability to adapt to change. Such a process needs to involve every member of the firm because employees are the best change agents in their respective areas of expertise. This process of creative iteration can be formalized into a simple set of steps, as Exhibit 3 shows:

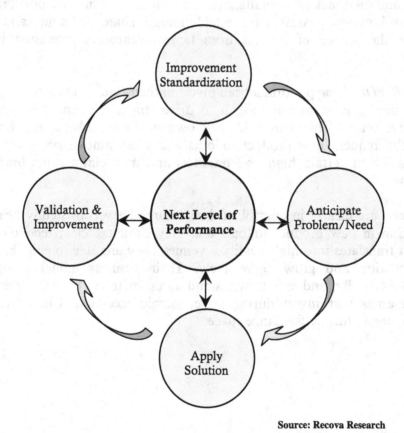

Source: Recova Research

Exhibit 3. Model for Continuous Adaptation Cycle

Step One. Anticipating needs or problem area

Continuous inspection of business processes may reveal areas where improvement may be effected. Evaluation of these processes against updated industry benchmark targets may reveal performance gaps perhaps not seen otherwise. Availability of new technologies or tools may provide paths for improvement. Similarly, expanded core competencies or fresh training may provide additional improvement options. The combination of new technologies, investment on training, core competence expansions, and new tools enable a sharper view into existing operations and subsequently, increase options for improvement.

Step Two. Finding a solution

Once the issue has been identified, investigated, documented, and an improvement option identified, a pilot implementation of a solution is usually a prudent approach. Nowadays, a pilot improvement should be designed more as validation of a previously simulated scenario rather than a total eye opener for those more complex problems. Computer simulation, as discussed in Chapter One, provides such a capability. In any case, a pilot approach would point the way toward a scalable solution.

Step Three. Validation of solution and improvement

The scalable solution can now be validated and implemented in large scale. Sometimes this is implemented in phases to accommodate production runs or product release schedules. Documentation and updated standards can now be created and training organized and delivered. Whatever regulatory requirements concerning these new procedures also need to be addressed at this time. Special care must be taken to ensure field personnel have been fully re-trained.

Step Four. Standardization of new solution

This is a phase for confirmation and assurance that all areas affected by the new solution have been addressed. At this time, the firm ensures that the resulting training, documentation, and regulatory compliance requirements have been fully met. This is not a phase to rest for a job well done; it is only a time to catch one's breath before starting the continuing adaptation cycle again. This can be effected through continuous vigilance on technology and industry advancements, analysis of competing product lines and product features, and analysis of changes in the business environment that could be harmful or beneficial to the firm, to name a few.

It is clear from this process that the firm must be committed at the enterprise level to support this ongoing search for improvement. This process does not preclude the adoption of disruptive technologies or the implementation of drastic change as authors Hammer and Champy argued in their book "Reengineering the Corporation", and more recently Champy in the book "X-Engineering the Corporation". In the dynamic enterprise environment there is a need, at different times, for different degrees of change. Experience has shown that both approaches can be valid for different situations. Our argument for a continuous approach to adaptation is based on our positive experience with organized, committed, and constant efforts toward performance improvement.

4.2 New Concepts Applicable To High Performance Financial Management

The source of revenue for any business is the customer. The high performance enterprise addresses the customer perspective in every detail in order to optimize its revenue generation. It is not outlandish to think of customers as "extended assets" of the enterprise, and from our perspective, high performance assets. This means that the customer base is not only a source of revenue but also knowledge we can tap to continuously improve our product portfolio, customer satisfaction level, and consequently, revenue.

Optimum knowledge about the customer would presumably guide our investment policy toward retaining and expanding the most profitable customer segments. Ideally, this would create a virtuous cycle of investment and profit that would significantly raise the enterprise's financial performance.

As we talk about product portfolios, the high performance enterprise will address its customer base as a Customer Portfolio where investment and product strategies are closely linked to long term customer satisfaction initiatives. We have already, in Chapter 3, examined the segmentation of a customer base as a function of profitability. Now we will include a risk factor that will refine our information for creating a Customer Portfolio. Knowledge regarding which customer segments will ensure steady and optimum financial return will be extremely useful in focusing our Customer Portfolio investment strategy.

4.2.1 Valuation Of A Customer Base In Terms Of Risk Factors

In conducting a valuation of a customer base assigning a risk factor associated with quality of revenue is extremely useful. This valuation would be included in the Extended Income statement as the Customer Relations item in the Cost of Extended Internal Capital Valuations section (Refer to the Management Extended Income Statement sample on page 78) and would provide a tangible estimate of the value of the customer base. This value can be used as a leading financial indicator for estimating future profitability. This could be of great value in determining an investment policy or for establishing a price for a potential acquisition.

From an enterprise perspective, increasing market share requires a careful evaluation of the actions of market leaders plus a well-crafted strategy of customer selection and product positioning designed to maximize the rate of returns earned on marketing investment.

As an example, consider the customer base profiles of Company X and company Y as are depicted in Exhibit 4. Each firm has a 40% market share and, even though their customer base profiles are very different, Company X and Company Y may, in the short term, have comparable income statements exhibiting very similar levels of profitability.

It might be tempting to infer that profitability is reflected equally in the profit margins for each category in the customer base, but that could be misleading. For example, Company X is investing its profits in order to increase its Share-determining customers (longer term payback), trying to reduce its number of

Switchable customers (by building barriers around certain accounts) and attempting to retain/increase its Loyal customers. As a result of those strategic investments, the current income statement of Company X shows modest profitability performance.

On the other hand, when an in-depth analysis of its customer base is completed, a high level of stability in revenue growth emerges, as well as bright future prospects for profitability. As Exhibit 4 illustrates, 45% of the customer base are Loyal and 18% are High-profit customers.

A detailed analysis of Company Y's customer base reveals a very different picture of the future. It has 8% of its customer-base in high profit, 7% in Share-determining, and 45% in Switchables. With this large percentage of Switchable customers, Company Y is liable to have a limited ability to tolerate adverse market conditions, leaving it vulnerable to producing flat or declining sales and sub-optimum profit margins.

Company X, on the other hand, has few Switchable customers in its customer base and therefore has created a position that allows it to invest more aggressively. In fact, Company X is a leading candidate to acquire the Switchable customers of Company Y (to leverage under-utilized assets at a profit, perhaps). Therefore, these two leading companies, with comparable market shares of 40% are very different when the value of their customer bases is fully investigated.

	High Profit	Share-Determining	Loyal	Switchable	Low-Profit	Total
Company X	18%	10%	45%	20%	7%	100%
Company Y	8%	7%	22%	45%	18%	100%

Exhibit 4: Customer Base Comparison of Two Companies

With this comparison in mind we will conduct a valuation of Company X's customer base to understand its dollar value. We create a risk factor associated with the revenue per customer type and the perceived continuity of sales as follows:

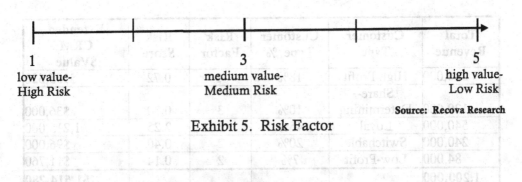

Source: Recova Research

Exhibit 5. Risk Factor

Next, we calculate the risk factor of the revenue by customer type as shown below for Company X. Note we multiply the customer type population percentage by the risk factor to obtain a risk score.

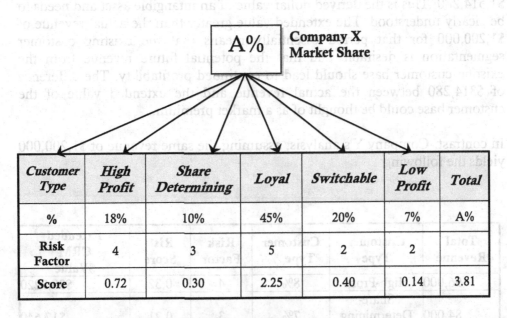

Customer Type	High Profit	Share Determining	Loyal	Switchable	Low Profit	Total
%	18%	10%	45%	20%	7%	A%
Risk Factor	4	3	5	2	2	
Score	0.72	0.30	2.25	0.40	0.14	3.81

Exhibit 6. Customer Distribution and Risk Factor

Now we introduce the revenue associated with customer type to calculate a dollar value for our Customer Relations entry in the Extended Income Statement.

Total Revenue	Customer Type	Customer Type %	Risk Factor	Risk Score	Extended CRM $Value
216,000	High-Profit	18%	4	0.72	$155,520
120,000	Share-Determining	10%	3	0.30	$36,000
540,000	Loyal	45%	5	2.25	$1,215,000
240,000	Switchable	20%	2	0.40	$96,000
84,000	Low-Profit	7%	2	0.14	$11,760
1,200,000					**$1,514,280**

Exhibit 7. Company X Valuation of Customer Base

According to this analysis, the extended value of the customer base is worth $1,514,280. This is the derived dollar value of an intangible asset and needs to be clearly understood. The extended value greater than the actual revenue of $1,200,000 for that period essentially means that the existing customer segmentation is desirable and that the potential future revenue from the existing customer base should lead to continued profitability. The difference of $314,280 between the actual revenue and the extended value of the customer base could be thought of as a market premium.

In contrast, Company Y's analysis, assuming the same revenue of $1,200,000 yields the following:

Total Revenue	Customer Type	Customer Type %	Risk Factor	Risk Score	Extended CRM $Value
96,000	High-Profit	8%	4	0.32	$30,7220
84,000	Share-Determining	7%	3	0.21	$17,640
264,000	Loyal	22%	5	1.1	$290,400
540,000	Switchable	45%	2	0.9	$486,000
216,000	Low-Profit	18%	2	0.34	$73,440
1,200,000					**$898,200**

Exhibit 8. Company Y Valuation of Customer Base

Company Y's extended value of the customer base is only $898,200. It is actually not a surprising valuation considering that most of the customers (45%) are on the Switchable category. Company Y's management is now alerted that continued profitability from this existing customer base is at risk. It follows that action should be taken to change the segmentation pattern of this customer base. This low valuation would indicate that a potential buyer of Company Y should not pay more than $898,200 for Company Y's customer base.

In conclusion, this example illustrates a way to conduct a customer base valuation utilizing a risk score associated with customer typology.

4.3 Extended Capital Management (ECM)

It is difficult to conduct a valuation of all tangible and intangible assets since traditional financial reports are based on fixed, or tangible assets. Generally accepted accounting principles (GAAP) have proven insufficient to accurately describe the total financial performance of an enterprise. Ascertaining the value of intangible assets such as intellectual capital, for example, is a problem that remains generally unresolved. Success of business strategies that emphasize tangible financial results from best practices depends greatly on the implementation of performance measurements that can gauge the ongoing impact of capital investment. This guide takes existing management systems and financial performance measurements as a reference and offers additional insight into developing measurement frameworks and internal financial reporting tools that increase visibility on the performance of enterprise assets.

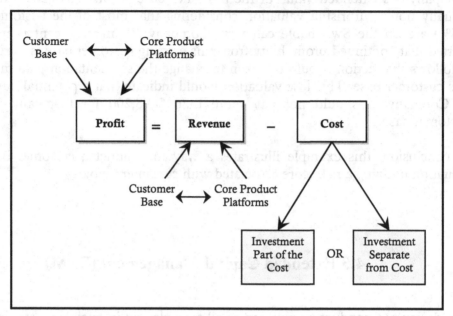

Exhibit 9: Strategic Renewal: Expense or Investment?

We call this additional perspective Extended Capital Management (ECM). It answers the management need to focus on the use of resources to create strategic and sustainable value for the enterprise. The Extended Balance Sheet and the Extended Income Statement are internal reporting tools that provide more visibility into the true value of the firm through the valuation of the firm's intellectual capital. They also separate expenses associated with assets that create long-term value from those required to sustain daily operations.

4.3.1 Economic Value Added (EVA)

A fundamental measure of a firm's performance is the ability to gain access to sources of external funding at competitive rates against which it can generate attractive returns. The measure of the markets perceived risk in the company is computed by taking the spread between the Return on Invested Capital (ROIC) and the risk-free cost of capital. In an economic period, normally a fiscal year, the performance of the company in one dimension is defined by its ability to meet or exceed a threshold of net operating income defined by its incremental earnings requirement on the capital managed by the business. The figure is obtained by multiplying the difference in rates by the capital outstanding at the beginning of the year (or the average over the year if that was used in computing the return on invested capital).

$$EVA = [ROIC(r) - Cost\ of\ Capital\ (c)] \times [Invested\ Capital]$$

A company's EVA [1], and thus its MVA (Market Value Added), can be increased in three different ways:

- By increasing the efficiency of existing operations, and thus the spread between (r) and (c);

- By increasing the amount of capital invested in projects where returns(r) are greater than costs (c);

- By withdrawing capital from operations where (r) is less than (c).

EVA is important in that it is the singular internal measure of a firm's performance to correlate to market value and, ultimately to market price.

There is a current view of EVA (depicted below) in use by the investment community. In this view the drivers of the operating decisions are:

- Sales Growth

- Operating Profit Margin

- Cash Income Tax Rate

Current View of EVA
Critical Value Drivers in Creating Shareholder Value

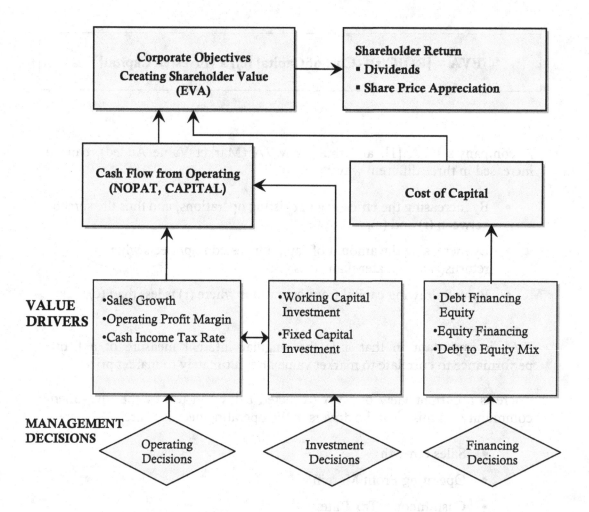

Exhibit 10. Current View of EVA

Essentially, EVA deals with acquiring and holding low-cost debt to improve profits and market value. Although useful, EVA's weakness is that it focuses on short-term financial gain, does not account for the value of intangible assets and disregards investment on long-term investment such as employee training, for example.

From an ECM perspective, EVA's Sales Growth and Operating Profit Margin are not the only drivers of the operating decisions. We can refine the EVA model by proposing an additional set of drivers for the operating decisions;

- Product Conformance
- Product Reliability
- Product Serviceability
- Cash Income Tax Rate

Where product conformance is a performance metric for assets that characterizes the degree to which a product's design and operating specifications match pre-designed standards. This difference is indicated by the capability indices Cp and Cpk. In the field service sector there are two common performance measures that deal with product performance. One is the incidence of service calls and the other, the frequency of repairs under warranty.

These new drivers of the operating decisions create the "extended view "of EVA, or EEVA. This method of assigning financial targets to the assets within a market segment is different than the approach used in a traditional reporting environment. Intangible assets are now accounted for and integrated into the strategic planning of the firm.

In many industries, the basis of competition requires the expenditure of significant funds to access or create scarce knowledge resources such as basic research, product design, manufacturing processes, production software, management systems, employee training, etc. These types of expenditures are treated by traditional financial accounting standards as intangibles and charged to current period expense. Pressure from the investment community on stock prices creates a motivation to show continued improvements in quarterly earnings results. Because "soft assets/strategic costs" are subtracted from sales revenues and therefore reduce profits, managers have strong incentives to deal with such expenditures on a short-term basis.

This proposed view, or Extended Capital Management, is in response to today's deficiencies in the valuation of enterprise assets. We expect that in the near future the ECM, along with a well-designed metrics framework that incorporates the value of intangible assets, will be a prerequisite for the high performance enterprise.

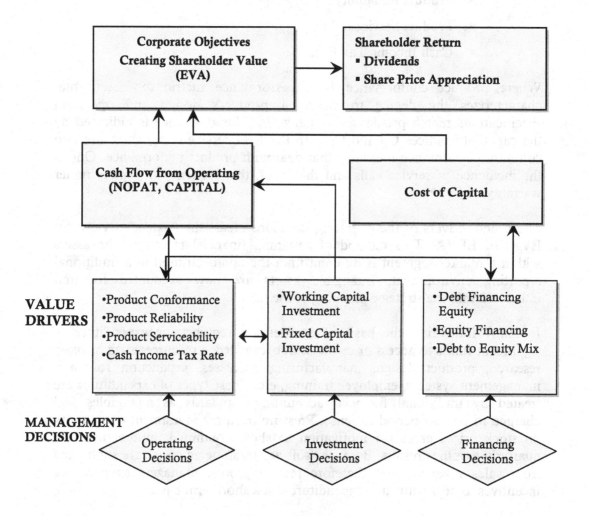

Extended EVA
Critical Value Drivers In Aligning Enterprise Assets With
Shareholder Value Creation

Exhibit 11. Extended EVA

4.4 New Financial Statement Aids

The previous sections of this guide have focused on the creation of a metrics framework to improve visibility on the financial performance of enterprise assets. Well-designed metrics frameworks will also ensure that asset performance is in alignment with the company's strategic objectives as indicated by the BSC methodology. We placed financial value on intangible assets in an effort to close the gap between market capitalization and book value and thus capture the true financial performance of the enterprise.

The need for management to focus on the optimum use of assets to create strategic value in the business suggests an additional form of review of periodic business expenses. The separation of those elements being used to create long-term value for the business from the expenses required to sustain daily operations can be portrayed in a fashion to identify long-term investments.

The Management Extended Income Statement

We will use the term "Management Extended Income Statement" to signify the operational impact of activities that segregate strategic and non-strategic financial factors.

The focus of the Management Extended Income Statement is to separate the contribution made by fixed assets of the business (e.g., manufacturing equipment) from intangible assets in order to highlight the true effect of market growth on profitability and the ability to fund additional strategic investments.

Also within this exhibit, overhead expenses such as Marketing, Sales, General and Administrative, R&D, and Interest on loans are combined and then partitioned into the strategic and non-strategic categories, again to evaluate the nature of the business value investment. Finally, environmental effects created by strategic initiatives for example, currency adjustments related to international expansion, are brought to the forefront of the analysis for management's immediate review.

As an element of the Management Extended Income Statement, significant period effects such as foreign currency adjustments and hedges can be included for more precise risk analysis. For instance, swings in the value of the dollar relative to other currencies can have a major impact on competitive position in industries involved in global markets. It is small consolation to be the most efficient enterprise in an industry if the advantage is wiped out by a 50 or 60 percent increase in the costs of goods consumed.

Management Extended Income Statement	$ (000)	%
REVENUE	$10,353	100.0%
COST OF GOODS SOLD		
Variable Costs	$3,493	33.7%
Costs Of Productive Fixed Assets	$1,282	12.4%
Costs Of Other Fixed Assets	$355	3.5%
Total	$5,130	49.6%
MARGINS		
Contribution	$6,860	66.3%
Productive Operating	$5,578	53.9%
Actual Operating	$5,223	50.4%
NON-MANUFACTURING EXPENSES		
Strategic	$1,216	11.7%
Non-Strategic	$2,856	27.6%
Total	$4,072	39.3%
Pre-Tax Profit Before Adjustments	$1,151	11.1%
Currency & Misc. Adjustments	$0	0.0%
Pre-Tax Profit	$1,151	11.1%

Exhibit 12. Management Extended Income Statement

The Management Extended Balance Sheet

The Management Extended Balance Sheet measures the assets that define a firm's competitive positioning. In the context of strategic value creation, such a composite measurement set would include:

- Quality of the firm's customer base (Customer segmentation)
- Customer satisfaction data
- Technological capabilities by platform
- Measurement of asset capability
- Productivity of tangible and intangible assets
- Benchmarking the company's innovation rate against significant competitors

The linking of the firm's total assets (product design, manufacturing process, supply chain, intellectual capital) through internal control systems like "Management Extended Income Statement" and "Management Extended Balance Sheet" creates a measurement for value creation within the firm. Further, these assets can be linked indirectly through Accounts Receivables to the customer types that they serve. With an analytic ability to measure and drive the intrinsic value of the business, comparisons to similar enterprises can be made. Specific metrics and relationships of value creation within the firm can be managed operationally.

Management Extended Balance Sheet	(000)
CURRENT ASSETS	$48,791
NET PROPERTY, PLANT & EQUIPMENT	$2,716
EXTENDED INTERNAL CAPITAL VALUATIONS:	
Technology	$346
Innovation	$113
Supplier Base Relations	$147
Productivity Of Assets	$65
Customer Base Relations	$434
Branding Of Products	$265
Management Of Human Capital	$2,546
(Split between Product Platforms and Administrative Functions)	
LESS: AMORTIZATION or CHANGE OF VALUE	$1,223
NET EXTENDED INTERNAL CAPITAL	$2,693
TOTAL EXTENDED CORPORATE ASSETS	$54,200
CURRENT LIABILITIES	$4,596
LONG-TERM LIABILITIES	$0
STOCKHOLDER'S EQUITY	
Common Stock	$222
Paid In Capital	$40,760
Retained Earnings	$5,929
Retained Value-Ext. Internal Capital	$2,693
TOTAL EXTENDED CORPORATE LIABILITIES AND STOCKHOLDER'S EQUITY	$54,200

Exhibit 13. Management Extended Balance Sheet

Conclusion

We were motivated in writing this guide by the awareness that, industry managers, in spite of investing tremendous amounts in IT and management systems still lack today the appropriate financial visibility to drive high performance firms. One looming concern is that business as usual will not be sufficient to thrive in global terms. Labor mobility and economic power migration will only add to the complexities of managing profitable firms in the future.

We need to substantially transform our expectations of business performance by the enterprise to ensure every element of the value chain is continually creating value for stakeholders. This applies not only to tangible or fixed assets; after all, efficiencies we can extract from machines and facilities are finite. Standardized valuation methods for intellectual capital must be developed and integrated into financial reporting by the high performance enterprise. The trend is toward increasing knowledge content of products and services, and human factors are important factors of a future competitive advantage that, we expect, will be based on innovation and high performance.

It is our hope that the information we have provided in this guide is helpful to our colleagues in establishing a framework for determining a more accurate value of the enterprise, including the value of intellectual assets. We started with providing sample metrics and a methodology for developing a metrics framework that could be utilized as scorecards. We showed how to segment and do a valuation of a customer base and how that could be applied to the supply chain and intellectual capital valuation. We ended this guide by integrating these factors into the Extended Capital Management model that, we hope, will motivate additional thought in driving the enterprise towards high performance.

Acknowledgements

We thank all our associates who provided assistance and encouragement in completing the Guide. Among them, special thanks to **Grace Red** for graphics and editing, and **Fay Sun Wong** for organization, digital design, and research.

GLOSSARY

AS IS	Initial phase of modeling a business process. It examines existing conditions.
BPA	Business Process Analysis, part of BPI.
BPI	Business Process Improvement
BSC	Balanced Scorecard, a management system for tracking strategic performance measures.
Cash Flow Velocity	The time it takes a dollar used to purchase/build a product to return as a customer payment, or the ratio of receivables & inventory less payables divided by the monthly cash receipts.
Cost of Capital	Capital refers to the money needed to keep an expanding enterprise operating and cost refers to the interest on that capital.
Cp	Capability is the term for processes or skills are in conformance with standards.
Cpk	This symbol represents the standard deviation of capability from the standard.
CRM	Customer Relationship Management or a series of processes to add value to or determine a value for existing customers.
DCF	Discounted Cash Flow
Driver	An operational control factor that influences the consistent value for costs.
Dynamic Simulation	The computer-based evaluation of multi-variable models.
ERP	Enterprise Resource Planning, software system to manage operations.
ECM	Extended Capital Management defines investments not measured by traditional financial measurements.

EVA	Economic Value Added, a financial measure, which is operating profits less the cost of all of the capital, employed to produce earnings.
EEVA	Extended Economic Value Added, the enterprise-wide asset alignment with shareholder value creation.
Extended Enterprise	The firm and its connections to suppliers and customers.
GAAP	Generally Accepted Accounting Principles, standard record keeping and reporting rules for U.S. firms.
IA	Intellectual Assets, values generated by performance metrics for intangible, non-product intellectual activities which add value to the enterprise.
IAM	Intangible Asset Monitor developed by Karl-Erik Svibey in 1987.
ICI	Intellectual Capital Index created by Intellectual Capital Services.
LCC	Life Cycle Costing or more closely measuring/projecting a product's life cycle.
Metrics	A series of standard algorithms using consistent measurements to determine a meaningful value.
Modeling	The act of creating or simulating diverse models.
MVA	Market Value Added is the difference between the Company's equity value as reported by GAAP versus current market value (Outstanding shares at market value).
NOPAT	Net Operating Profit After Taxes
NPV	Net Present Value
OEM	Original Equipment Manufacturer or a market maker through which products are distributed to establish an expanding market presence.
PLC	Product Life Cycle
R	Replacement Cost Valuation

ROA	Return On Assets
ROIC	Return On Invested Capital, net operating profit divided by invested capital.
RP	Risk Projection
SCM	Supply Chain Management or enterprise systems to manage logistics and inputs and outputs of the enterprise.
SCOR	Supply Chain Operations Reference model defined by the Supply Chain Council, an industry organization.
Six Sigma	A management rating system utilizing variations from the standard performance. For example, one sigma equals 70 flaws per 100 repetitions whereas six sigma equals .0003 flaws per 100 repetitions.
Strategy Wheel	How different elements of a strategy form a hub and the spokes that move the enterprise forward.
T	The cost of money (capital) for one year.
TO BE	A prototype or proposed business model or process.
TCO	Total Cost of Ownership or how an asset contributes to or subtracts from an enterprise.

INDEX

W

X

Y

Z

Printed in the United States
By Bookmasters